The Psychologist's Guide
to an Academic Career

HARRIET L. RHEINGOLD

American Psychological Association
Washington, DC

Published by
American Psychological Association
750 First Street, NE
Washington, DC 20002

Copies may be ordered from
APA Order Department
P.O. Box 2710
Hyattsville, MD 20784

In the United Kingdom and Europe, copies may be ordered from
American Psychological Association
3 Henrietta Street
Covent Garden
London WC2E 8LU
England

Typeset in Goudy by Easton Publishing Services, Inc., Easton, MD

Printer: Data Reproductions Corporation, Rochester Hills, MI
Cover designer: Berg Design, Albany, NY
Technical/production editor: Valerie Montenegro

Library of Congress Cataloging-in-Publication Data

Rheingold, Harriet L. (Harriet Lange)
    The psychologist's guide to an academic career / Harriet L. Rheingold.
        p.   cm.
    Includes bibliographical references and index.
    ISBN 1-55798-227-9 (acid-free paper)
    1. Psychology—Practice.   I. Title.
    BF75.R445   1994
    150'.23—dc20   94-532
                                                                CIP

British Library Cataloguing-in-Publication Data
A CIP record is available from the British Library.

Printed in the United States of America
First edition

CONTENTS

iii

FOREWORD

When I heard of this book, during its incubation while I was science director of the American Psychological Association (APA), it was apparent that the APA must publish it. The book would surely improve the quality of life for graduate students and new faculty members in psychology and would also provide exceptional wisdom and administrative guidance for more experienced scholars, especially those responsible for enhancing the quality of graduate programs. Now that I have read the book, I see that I was right!

Child developmentalists are familiar with the phenomenon of "ghosts in the nursery," an expression suggesting that as new parents begin caring for their children, their own earlier experiences, particularly with their parents, are powerful influences in setting the agenda. The tone of the new relationship and issues of how the child's training will be carried out will be affected by remembrances of things past, or historical echoes.

Early child training is concerned largely with conveying to the child what is prohibited or must be inhibited and, not less important, what is permitted. Much of child rearing is a matter of shaping desired behaviors in acceptable ways, giving advice, and instilling self-regulated discipline. The ways in which the shaping takes place and the manner of the tutor are of as much importance as the substance of the directive.

The work of a seasoned and successful academician whose personal generosity and professional largess have prompted her to impart her wisdom to beginning scholars, this book could well serve for decades as an inner voice for psychologists in training or at the start of their careers. While promoting high academic goals, Rheingold exudes respectful nurturance of the willing scholar entering the academic profession. Because of the beauty of expression so characteristic of its author throughout her career, the volume could serve as a companion piece to Strunk and White's *Elements of Style*. This "likeness" is apt, for Rheingold reveals she first encountered *Elements of Style* in 1924, when she studied at Cornell with Strunk. Her own early training took, and Rheingold is still listening carefully to her own mentors, just as she implores her readers to listen to theirs.

In writing an advice book for budding psychologists seeking academic careers and participating in the scholarly life, Rheingold could give the impression that progress is linear. However, she herself arrived, like many outstanding scholars, over a circuitous route. She was first a clinical psychologist, then a teacher in a small college, and then she went on to a "late PhD" at the University of Chicago. Rheingold began her postdoctoral career as a child development and behavior specialist in one of the major national research institutes and only then went on to the University of North Carolina, where she was a distinguished professor.

Because she is one of the most accomplished and versatile research psychologists and teachers of our day, Professor Emeritus Rheingold's revelations are themselves a reassuring start to her book. Although it might seem that such a volume would read like a "how to do it" treatise or a Boy Scout manual for instant success in the scholarly way of life, what we have here is an homage to diversity and thoughtful pathfinding for individuals. Most academicians, thankfully, are pioneers and dare to travel new roads. Rheingold provides insights into the social structure of the university and of the academic way of life that foster such personal creativity in a spirit of group enterprise.

This is not a book for novices alone. I found myself transported to aspects of my own earlier career in reading it, and as I read, I thought, in several places, that I could have used her advice beneficially. Guaranteed to spark recollections in seasoned academicians, this is a book for veteran scholars to savor. Rheingold has written a "Reminiscences" as much as she has written a guide for the beginner.

One is touched by Rheingold's recitation of incidents in her life, as when she was invited to march, in full academic regalia, in an awesome procession, with scholars representing universities founded as long ago as the twelfth century. She reflects, "At that moment I sensed the meaning of a community of scholars. . . ." It is that community of scholars to which Rheingold welcomes the reader, younger and older, and with that welcome, she reminds us of our responsibilities, our hopes for the future, our fears, our regrets, and the fun.

LEWIS P. LIPSITT
Brown University

PREFACE

A VOICE FROM THE
IVORY TOWER

I have written this book to advise those who aspire to a career of teaching, research, and service in psychology. At first, I envisioned it as notes to my students, but over the years my students grew up to be scholars, scientists, professors, and public servants, and I, too, advanced in years to emeritus status. Although they are still in my mind, and I write as though they still sit across the desk from me, now I write for all persons as they live through the stages of a career I here portray—indeed, as they live a life of learning and service.

For all who study behavior, then, the book starts with your early days in graduate school, carries you through the many steps of your career, and concludes with advice on how to organize your day and your life. Although I write as a psychologist and often draw on the guidelines of the American Psychological Association (APA), the issues I treat are general enough to apply to students and scholars in the wider scope of the behavioral sciences.

The advice is practical and offers what I hope is sage counsel, even if given in seemingly pedestrian detail at places. The book was written not for geniuses who write their own rules, but for ordinary toilers in the vineyard, among whom I count myself, who struggle with uncertainties that seem never to trouble the geniuses. As often as I find the autobiographies of great scholars and scientists inspiring and exhilarating, just as often I find their achievements intimidating. I am hoping that nothing in my advice will be intimidating and that all of it will be within your abilities.

With time and experience you would have learned by yourself much of what I here present. I write to provide that knowledge for you *now*. Even though my behavior did not follow my own good counsel as often as I wished it had, that is not sufficient reason for your slackening. My advice may read as though I had some special access to Reason and Conscience, when in fact I write out of Experience. And if at times I seem to be a stern mentor, I do mean to be such a one.

Although much of my advice pertains to teaching, research, scholarly works, and service in a university, it applies as well to positions in liberal arts colleges where teaching carries greater emphasis and to positions in institutes that engage primarily in research. In fact, many people move freely from one type of institution to another with advantage and without penalty. Students and professors alike should recognize that no position closes the door to any other. You will live longer than you can now imagine, and, over a lifetime, careers can develop in many different ways.

Sense and order in a career's development often can be seen only in retrospect. Thus, I now make sense of and find order in my own unorthodox career: 8 years in a child guidance clinic (yes, as a clinical psychologist!), as many years again teaching in a small liberal arts college for women, a late PhD degree, and 8 years in a research institute, before a position in a university. From such a history you might conclude that I do not have the credentials to offer advice that in some particulars did not guide my own career. Nevertheless, that history justifies my conviction that many avenues are open to achievement and none fixes one's career unalterably. Change is possible, and each avenue provides experiences valuable to the next.

Although the times may not seem especially propitious for a life in academe, openings for postdoctoral training continue and research institutes proliferate. Still, there are openings for professors, scholars, and investigators in psychology and the behavioral sciences, and in only a few years there well may be a shortage of professors when many current faculty members retire. No matter, there will always be room for the dedicated. I remain firm in my conviction that teaching, scholarship, research, and service qualify as personally rewarding, universally respected, and, all in all, noble endeavors.

Thus, I have set forth a few principles of behavior that can stand you in good stead no matter how the times may change. As Cobbett said, "It is the duty, and ought to be the pleasure of age and experience, to warn and instruct youth, and to come to the aid of inexperience."[1] Cobbett used the metaphor of the "placing of buoys and of lights," which I often thought a fitting title for my advice. True, the tenor of my advice is idealistic and optimistic and may be faulted by some as unrealistic in places, a tenor undoubtedly influenced by what has seemed to me to be my own fortunate

---

[1] From *Advice to Young Men, and (Incidentally) to Young Women* (p. 1) by W. Cobbett, 1830/1980, Oxford: Oxford University Press.

experience. Nevertheless, I staunchly defend my faith in the system under which my colleagues and I perform our duties.

A word about this Preface's title: Let no one think that I use the term *ivory tower* unmindful of its dictionary definition as a secluded place where practical issues are treated with an impractical, often escapist attitude. No, I use the term in defiance of the dictionary to define what it means to me and, I believe, to my fellow inhabitants of campuses everywhere. Of course, I could say with Humpty-Dumpty that when I use a word, it means just what I choose it to mean. But as I look about me, I see my colleagues engaged in great endeavors, searching for the truth and for ways to improve the human condition. Indeed, in the ivory tower, every clash of ideas occupies center stage—today, health care, tomorrow, civil rights, and the day after, crime and violence. Let yesterday's words serve yesterday's language; no longer should Sainte-Beuve's use of the term more than a century ago tarnish the splendid image of today's colleges and universities. It is time to add a new definition of the ivory tower: a tower, yes, to rise above shallow and selfish concerns and thus to gain the larger view, and ivory, too, because special and valued. So, the voice from the ivory tower—my voice—is not divorced from the sternest reality; rather, it is the essence of that reality.

In writing these pages, I returned again and again to Pavlov's advice to the youth of his country, written in 1936 when he was 87 years old. In some 250 words he urged students, first, to be strictly systematic in the acquisition of knowledge, to practice self-restraint and patience, and to penetrate into "the mystery" of the origin of facts. His second important requisite was modesty: "Never at any time imagine that you know everything. No matter how highly you are appreciated by others, have the courage to say to yourself, 'I am ignorant.'"[2] He ended his statement with a call for passion in one's work and search for truth. Now, as I read his legacy to students once again, I think that here I only spell out in detail what he wrote so stirringly in so few words.

In appreciation, I thank Robert T. Brown, Gerald A. Doyle, Don W. Hayne, Lewis P. Lipsitt, Alberta Siegel, and Meredith J. West, who encouraged me in preparing these words; Lynne Baker-Ward, James O. Freedman, Josh Haskett, Don W. Hayne, Lyle V. Jones, William H. Redd, Ross Vasta, and Meredith J. West, whose interesting and valuable contributions expanded the scope of these pages; the chancellors of my university and the heads of my department, who provided, and now long after my retirement continue to provide, a congenial environment in which to bring these efforts to fruition; Carolyn Bloomer, Vicki Fowler, and Julia A. McVaugh,

---

[2] From *Pavlov, a Biography* (p. 110) by B. P. Babkin, 1949, Chicago: University of Chicago Press.

who conscientiously brought my manuscript to the printed page; Julia Frank-McNeil, Theodore J. Baroody, and Valerie Montenegro, the APA editors who skillfully moved the manuscript to publication; and, above all, my students, whose sensitive response to my teachings provided the occasion for writing this book.

I

PREPARING FOR AN ATTRACTIVE PROFESSION

1

BEING A GRADUATE STUDENT

Why should you spend so many years of your life preparing for an academic career in psychology, working so hard, and meeting such seemingly impossible standards as I shall set forth? Because it is an attractive profession, a profession that marks you as a learned person, doing important work that is respected by all serious people and thereby adding to that precious commodity, the world's future intellectual capital. You teach an area of knowledge and you contribute to it. You elevate reason above prejudice, affect generations of students, and influence events far beyond the classroom.

Given the importance of such a profession, its other attractive features are amazing. High among them is the freedom it affords. In the classroom you are free to teach what you think important and to do so in the manner you think most beneficial to your students. In your office or laboratory you are free to work on any scholarly task you deem worthy. You can call established facts into question and propose new ones—indeed, you should. Your freedom to think and to speak is matched by the freedom to spend your unscheduled hours as best suits your needs and obligations. In any day, you need no one's permission to read journals in the library, to revise your class notes, to write the opening paragraph of an essay, or to prepare a grant proposal. During any vacation or leave you can teach or study or work in a clinic, a research institute, or a government agency.

3

These freedoms accompany another remarkable power of this attractive profession—the power to determine, together with your colleagues, the character and reputation of your department and institution as well as the curriculum of the students (with due respect to deans, provosts, chancellors, and trustees).

For these freedoms the obligations are correspondingly great, but nevertheless welcome because they are what you would anyway most want to do: to learn more, to help others, and to behave honorably. This is what the rest of this book is about.

To prepare for that attractive profession, you enter a graduate program of study—a serious, demanding, and exciting venture. You are committing yourself to a profession and a discipline; so, too, are the professors and the university committing themselves to help you realize your goal. Within this alliance, you recognize the professors as the arbiters of your progress; the professors, for their part, see in their students the legatees of their vision and principles; and it is the university that makes the alliance possible— a silent but indispensable partner.

PROFESSORS AND COURSES

To enrich the value of each course you take, learn the academic background of your professors, their research interests, their scientific orientation, and the tradition they represent. They are products of their training and experience, just as you will be. In the directories of the American Psychological Association (APA), the American Psychological Society (APS), and other professional societies, you can find out where your professors received their degrees and where they taught before joining your department. In the lectures they give and the papers they write, you will hear echoes of their mentors, as later will be true of your own lectures and papers. In the process, you are acquiring a history of scholarship and science, of theory and thought. You are constructing an intellectual family tree that will mark your own future place.

Beyond the required courses these professors teach, look for possibilities to broaden your background. As your schedule permits, take (or at least audit) courses in biology—evolution, genetics, and the neurosciences—and especially in mathematics. Many of you, especially women, may have shunned math. Yet the evidence points to your ability to master it, and for all of us that subject, above all, has been held to add the most power to our thinking. You also will profit from some knowledge of other forces shaping your life. Make space, then, for some courses in the humanities, especially in ethics and philosophy, to see the role of sciences in the larger scheme of things. Finally, don't sneer at courses in writing and speaking; you need all the help you can get. Consult your professors, of course, and be adventuresome.

THE TASK OF READING

Reading will consume countless hours of your time in graduate school. How can you spend those hours more productively? First, try to fathom how the authors define their terms—a special problem in psychology, which uses such everyday terms as *intelligence*, *anxiety*, *experience*, and *learning*. Whenever you come across such a word, a flag should rise in your mind and stay aloft until you are sure of the meaning the author ascribes to it.

Then, try to think of yourself as entering into a colloquy with the writer. What is the writer's question, and what is the answer? How good is the evidence and how sound the reasoning? At the same time, widen the scope of your inquiry and ask, "Where did the question come from, and does the evidence support or contradict the facts and theories I already know?" If you are following my advice, you are evaluating the article's contribution to your knowledge and pondering its significance.

Still, reading is but the first part; taking notes is the second. High-lighting passages (assuming you own the book or article) is not note taking, nor is photocopying. In taking notes, the hand assists the eye, and your attention is thereby assured. Try to handle each reference only once, exactly and completely; try, I say, because all too easily the eye glazes over, the mind dozes, and the head nods. Instead, rehearse the main facts, say them to yourself, and, as soon as possible, discuss them with someone else, all in an attempt to fix a clear and sharp memory.

Reading a Book

To get the clearest understanding of a scientific book quickly and efficiently, do not start on page 1. The natural tendency to do so might bog you down at about page 26, to judge from the prolific, often crude, and always sacrilegious underlining and notes in the margin that stop at just about that page in the books I withdraw from the library. Not only have these "readers" committed a crime, but they have learned little about the book.

Contrary to that natural tendency, start by reading the foreword and the preface. From those few pages you learn what the authors intend and who their mentors and colleagues were so that you can place the book within that tradition and stream of knowledge I alluded to earlier. Next, study the chapter headings to learn the main themes and to foresee how the author will proceed to develop them. Now, you are prepared to read the first chapter and then the last. Together with the chapter headings, these will give you a fairly complete idea of the book as a whole. If now you have more time, read the first and last paragraphs of the intermediate chapters, and peruse the index. Indeed, an index can be even more useful than chapter headings in revealing the main thrust of the book.

Thus, in a couple of hours, you will have mastered the main thrust of the book, savored the author's style, assigned the book a place in the panoply of knowledge, and gauged its relevance for your interests. (I hope my advice dismays no author who spent hours, weeks, and years crafting every sentence, but at least I did get your readers past page 26.)

Reading a Journal Article

A report of empirical research follows a time-honored order, from Introduction to Discussion, but here, too, as in reading a book, you can alter the order in which you read (and study) its parts, and do so with profit. To get your bearings, read the abstract and the first paragraph of the Introduction. Then turn directly to the Method. Who were the subjects: mice or men, old or young, and how many? What were their previous experiences? Indeed, the characteristics of the subjects set the stage for all that follows. Still, that is not enough, because you must know how this sample of subjects was selected from the available population so that you can weigh its effect on the generalizability of the results. Next, where was the study conducted, how were the subjects prepared or instructed, what measures were taken, and how were they analyzed?

Now you are ready to study the findings. Spend time on the tables and figures, and work out the statistical tests, at least in principle. The results lead naturally into the Discussion. Read the first paragraph, and read it again, to learn what the researcher considered the study's main findings. Then, as you read the next paragraph, turn to the Introduction, and from this point on, work through both sections in turn.

Why did I postpone your studying the Introduction? First, knowing the method and results, you can evaluate how successfully the researcher answered the question posed in the first paragraph of the Introduction; by itself, the Introduction cannot be taken as evidence that the question will be answered. Second, by comparing the Discussion and Introduction, you can judge how well the results supported, corrected, or extended the findings and theories of earlier investigators. I am not implying that the statement of the question and its history are not important; rather, I am emphasizing the importance of data. Theories wax and wane, but data survive—for a long time.

THE TASK OF WRITING

Reading takes time and effort, but writing takes a great deal more. To read the thoughts of others is as nothing compared with putting your own into words. We are advised that good writing is simple, clear, and precise. Yet the ease with which this advice can be stated belies the extent of the work required to follow it. In fact, you can accept Jacques Barzun's (1983) statement that "a wording that really exhausts the author's intention comes only from effort that exhausts the author too" (p. 44).

Although it is given to few to write deathless prose, all of us can learn to write better. To become sensitive to the rhythm of a good sentence, dip into some good writing now and again—something short and not too distracting—perhaps E. B. White's essays. Then, aids to good writing abound and you can read them as much for pleasure in their well-formed sentences and paragraphs as for instruction. For example, H. W. Fowler cannot be equaled for crispness, wit, and irony; open his *Modern English Usage* (1926) anywhere and be the wiser. Add to it *The Elements of Style* (Strunk & White, 1959) fashioned by E. B. White on William Strunk's original paperbound little book, which I bought for 25 cents in 1924 when I studied under Professor Strunk at Cornell University. To turn ordinary prose into clear, powerful, and effective writing, Joseph M. Williams (1990) has much good advice. Above all, indeed *primus inter pares*, consult the *Publication Manual of the American Psychological Association* (1983); because it presents the accepted form for all written papers and journal articles, study it from your first days in graduate school, and anticipate that you will refer to it a thousand times in your career.

To refresh my own efforts to write better, I often turn to the opening sentence of Franklin D. Roosevelt's broadcast to the nation on March 12, 1933 (Buhite & Levy, 1992). It was the ninth day of his presidency; the banks had been closed for a week to halt a panic among depositors, and the unemployed were selling apples on street corners. He began, "I want to tell you what has been done in the last few days, why it was done, and what the next steps are going to be" (p. 12). Every time I read those words, I envision a stirring outline for an article.

Writing Essays

Under the term *essays* I include all the papers you are asked to write, the short and long ones and the term papers. Whether the topic is assigned or of your choice, it is bound to be more complex than it seems at first; to grasp its full import, give it careful thought. Then, because psychology's vocabulary contains so many everyday words, you must not wobble from paragraph to paragraph in the meaning you assign to such terms as *thinking*, *remembering*, and *learning*, to say nothing of *fear*, *aggression*, and *envy*.

In the usual order, present your main idea first; then, paragraph by paragraph, weigh the evidence in its support, evaluate alternative views, show the implication of that main idea for theory or practice, and in the last paragraph draw the argument to a close by summarizing the main points and their relation to your opening statement.

In citing evidence, you must be punctilious in giving credit to others for their findings, ideas, and words. Not to do so is plagiarism. Then, be sure to give credit to the person who first enunciated the concept or who first conducted the research that opened a new area, even if you also cite an up-to-date review article of work that builds on it. And, in weighing evidence, be wary of citing a secondary source, that is, someone's version of a primary source (e.g., what William James, Freud, or Skinner said); often incomplete and inaccurate, the interpretation well might not be your own, had you read the original. Finally, be judicious in the number of quotations you use—wondrous as quotations are, strive for your own words.

Writing Examinations

Here, I am referring to examinations written in class that ask you to answer several questions (to discuss, compare, or evaluate—that is, "thought" questions) such as occur in midterm or final examinations or in the larger set of comprehensive examinations often required to gauge your general competence for proceeding through the graduate program. They are really a series of essays to be written on the spot. Tension mounts as you read the questions, and your natural impulse is to start writing at once. Resist the impulse. Unnerving as it may be to hear everyone around you busily scratching away, abstain.

Instead, read *all* the questions slowly and deliberately to grasp exactly what each asks. As in writing a paper on a required topic, be alert to the complexity inherent in most questions about behavior. Then, in any order jot down notes on all the questions; because they are just for yourself, use any part of speech—nouns, verbs, or names, even abbreviations and symbols. As you work on one question, ideas for answering another will come to mind; add these to your notes. Thus, as you work along, you will discover that you do know more than you thought you did on the first reading of even the difficult questions (such as the one that initially evokes the despair of total ignorance).

Now, to get off to a good start, choose the easiest question, order its notes in your mind, and only then begin to write. Each answer, of course, takes the form of an essay, presenting your main ideas in an introductory paragraph, supporting them in succeeding paragraphs, and concluding with a review of the main points.

To follow my advice requires discipline and faith in the powers of your mind. I am asking you to take valuable time just to think and make notes. Still, be assured that while you do that, some of your fellow students will be discovering when halfway through the first question—just as you might have—that they should have attacked the question in quite some other way; and then later, when answering the second, third, or fourth question, they will suddenly realize how they should have answered the first. You, in contrast, will be submitting a series of well-organized answers, and one of them just might present an argument so original and creative that the professor had not yet thought of it.

Writing Theses and Dissertations

These important documents are also written in the language of scholars and scientists and are prepared not only for your professors but also to meet the technical requirements of your graduate school. Because in most of these documents you are reporting on empirical research, take as your first guide the advice of the APA *Publication Manual* on preparing an article for publication. See also Cone and Foster (1993) and my chapter 10 in this volume. You may then depart from these guidelines, but cautiously, in some acceptable ways: You are usually permitted to present a more extensive, although still selective, review of the literature; you may give a more detailed description of your method and procedures; and you are allowed more freedom in speculating about the meaning of your findings, and in proposing plans for future work. Even raw data can find a place in an appendix, together with details of the apparatus and evidence of approval by ethical boards.

In envisioning these documents early on as journal articles, you will gain by adopting a simple, sparse, and precise style, and you will ease the always difficult task of one day preparing them for publication.

DEGREE REQUIREMENTS

Early and late, pore over the requirements for graduation—those of the graduate school, the department, and your area of concentration within the department. Of special interest are the nature and timing of written and oral examinations, the research and teaching requirements, the composition of examining committees, and the time limits for obtaining the master's and doctoral degrees. Throughout, the various documents warn that the responsibility for satisfying the requirements rests with you, the so-called degree candidate.

The Research Requirement

By considering the research requirement after the tasks of reading and writing, I do not mean to imply that fulfilling it waits on them. Quite the contrary! Almost from the day you enter graduate study, how you will fulfill this requirement occupies your thoughts. (And, no matter how inexperienced you feel, you, like all of us—and I could be talking about myself today—dream of making an earthshaking discovery.) Although all departments require a doctoral dissertation, and some also a master's thesis as preliminary, all expect students to engage in research during each year of study. What differs year by year is the demand for increasing degrees of originality and independence.

In the beginning, cast about for some agreement between your own interests and the research activities and theoretical orientations of the professors in the department. Gradually, from the courses they teach, and from informal conversations with them and the students, you will form a preference and then approach a likely professor with your idea. Or, you may volunteer (or have already agreed) to serve as a research assistant, perhaps with compensation, on a professor's research project, and in that way you may find an advisor with congenial interests.

Over days and weeks, you formulate a question and testable hypotheses. You read more about the topic and talk about it with fellow students and with professors. You refine the question and sharpen the hypotheses, omit a variable, alter another, and expand still a third. You go home discouraged at night but start the process again the next morning. You may give up the idea, pick up another, and even shift to another advisor. But all along, whatever the topic, pursue only those questions of burning interest to you—no less will do.

In the meantime, you are learning the principles governing the ethical treatment of human and nonhuman research subjects and the need for your proposal to be approved by the department's ethics committee and the university's institutional review board. Indeed, they may call for still more revisions before you can even try out your idea in pilot studies.

Then, semester by semester, your research hypotheses become more clear-cut and penetrating as you profit from courses in experimental design and statistical theory. So, too, you become aware of your obligation to honor the tenets of scientific integrity. And, as your research becomes more and more yours alone, your efforts are scrutinized by increasingly larger committees of professors; demanding and conflicting as their advice may be, you never again will have so much wisdom at your command.

However small your research project, it will cost money—money for travel to and from subjects, video- and audiotaping, food and bedding for animals, toys for children, and computer costs. Some of these items may come from your professors' grants, if your research is closely related to theirs, and some from the university. But beyond your campus, many agencies, public and private, and many professional and learned societies have money set aside to support dissertation research, some especially earmarked for women and minority persons. The rub is that many such grants are competitive, but you gain by having to compose a grant proposal, thereby developing a researcher's indispensable skill. Small though these amounts may be, they can signify the first public recognition of your efforts; many investigators in later years testify to the encouragement and inspiration the awards offered at a crucial time in their career. For information on these opportunities, consult your student financial aid office.

The Teaching Requirement

More and more universities require that candidates participate in teaching, at levels of independence varying from assisting a professor to carrying full responsibility for a class. Such a class would generally be a smallish one (about 35 to 50 students), at the undergraduate level, and in your area of concentration.

Besides satisfying a requirement for the degree, teaching may provide useful financial support. Teaching also teaches you, and thus you profit by the increased knowledge and the new ideas evoked by your students' questions. Furthermore, many tenure-track positions for assistant professors not only require prior teaching experience but also ask for student evaluations of your performance.

How can you manage to take courses, write papers, pass examinations, do research, *and* teach? Indeed, to teach just one course can be an absorbing full-time job for a novice. First off, pare your schedule to a minimum. Put your research on hold, or keep it barely simmering. Postpone difficult courses, and instead take a course in scientific writing or public speaking, or audit a course in philosophy or ethics. Try to attend a workshop on teaching at an APA or APS convention or, closer to home, spend a few hours with the people in your campus center on learning and teaching, and consult their books for useful tips. Then, scan chapter 4 in this volume, but do not labor over it this early in your career.

In sum, expect teaching to take time, close attention, and much effort. Accept as normal the good teacher's nagging urge to become a still better teacher. Then, teach the *students*, not the course, by which I mean do not just read your notes aloud. On all counts you will be a better teacher; the students will learn more, and you will have better student evaluations to offer your new employer.

BEING A MEMBER OF A PROFESSION

Even while you are still a graduate student, you can step into the world of your profession by joining a professional society—for example, the APA. Joining will pay you handsome dividends. You need pass no exams, write no papers, but for only a small amount of money, you become a member of a profession and catch a view of your future. Through the society's publications you learn of upcoming meetings, calls for papers, opportunities for further study, job openings, and the profession's continuing efforts to refine its code of ethical behavior. You see, too, all the concerns of a profession as it tries to solve the nation's and the world's problems.

On some occasion, you may consider attending a meeting—starting perhaps with a regional one rather than the national convention. You see and hear the scholars whose work you have long studied, and you learn of new developments as they are being made. You can have a stimulating exchange with the presenter of a poster on a problem close to your own research. Then, browsing the exhibits of new books and apparatus is sure to give you an idea or two to improve your teaching or benefit your research. And, from time to time, tag along with one or another of your professors who can introduce you to important persons. (Inquire of their assent, of course, but generally your presence will be welcome.) Yes, travel to meetings costs money, but if you have won a place on the program, you may qualify for assistance from your university or society.

THE RETURNING STUDENT

Although almost all graduate students are uncertain of their ability to succeed, should you return after a period away you are even more uncertain—fearing the competition from the younger students and, even more, the blunting of your academic skills. Paradoxically, at the same time you may think that your accumulated experience of working and living deserves some credit and surely ought to enhance your efforts. Indeed it does, because you now have more knowledge of the world outside and, above all, a clearer sense of purpose.

Be prepared to discover that what was a simple fact in an undergraduate course is in a graduate course a complex set of concepts. Be prepared, too, for a certain amount of work that at first may seem dry and irrelevant, something that undergraduates tend to accept with less complaint. On balance, though, my advice to this point fails to prepare you for the hours of work entailed; at the end of the day, you can walk away from a job, but you cannot from your studies. Prepare, also, for a reduced standard of living; what a person can afford on a reasonable salary becomes luxuries a student cannot. Fortunately, the academic environment sets small store on worldly goods. Much more serious may be your continuing responsibilities for spouse and children; you will need their support for the sacrifices and compromises that lie ahead.

Despite the cautionary tenor of my advice, it should intimidate no returning student. Those who returned to school under the G.I. Bill during the 1940s proved to be especially able and dedicated. So, too, are today's returning students, you among them.

HOW LONG WILL IT TAKE?

Traditionally, universities set forth, at least on paper, a 4-year program of study and research for the PhD. Yet many students take a great deal longer. Some must take time to earn money, often serving as research assistants. Some teach to gain experience or to satisfy a requirement, and teaching can usurp all other pursuits. Courses can be taken, papers written, research proposals prepared and approved, and data gathered and summarized but, in the end, the writing of the dissertation may drag on unconscionably. Or so it seems.

Do not let that happen, but push to obtain the degree as fast as you can. First, obtaining it provides a great sense of accomplishment. Then, the degree opens doors to many and new possibilities. Never fear, the degree is not the end of learning; faced by the demands of a new position, you will learn more than if you had stayed on as a student.

What can you do to move your dissertation to completion? Unless your need is dire, do not work to earn money; instead, seek financial aid or obtain a loan, and in any case, reduce your standard of living. And, if you are mired in doubt, go to a professional meeting to rejuvenate your resolve. If you cannot see what to do next, read the latest issue of a journal to find a clue in the work of others. Above all, press your professors for their attention.

In the end, graduate study, albeit a great experience, is also a source of great anxiety. You are painfully aware of how little you know, and you constantly question your ability to succeed. Your classmates, as bright as you, serve as discomforting comparisons for your own achievements. You stand in awe of those a few years ahead of you and pore over the dissertations of recent graduates with wonder at their brilliance. Will you ever do as well? Persevere, and you will.

2

FINDING A POSITION

Even before you settle on a dissertation topic, you will have begun to think about life after graduate school. What will be your first position? It would be nice if someone just offered you one—for example, a tenure-track position as an assistant professor—but you cannot expect, as you might have in days past, to obtain a position by word of mouth alone. Today, by the rules of affirmative action, all openings must be advertised and all candidates considered. Therefore, you cannot wait to be discovered but must exert yourself to find openings.

Some notices of openings are sent to your professors and are posted on the department's bulletin boards. A wider array appear in monthly issues of the *APA Monitor* and the *APS Observer* and at the placement offices of the regional and national conventions of these and other professional societies. Look also at the *Chronicle of Higher Education* for occasional listings.

Many factors guide your efforts. The first is a practical and often overriding one: the need to support yourself. Then, you will consider which of several possibilities best serves to establish the career you have in mind; that I call the professional factor. As important are many personal factors: your preferences for different parts of the country and kinds of communities, and especially your ties to other near and dear persons and your responsibilities for them.

Whatever the position for which you apply (later on I describe several types), first consult your professors who know not only you and your interests and abilities but also much about the position. They know, if only by reputation, the institution's philosophy, standards, and achievements and the nature of the student body. Seek their advice as you begin your search, and continue to do so at every step. Second, take the time to visit your campus's office of career planning for more general advice on conducting a successful job search, and see also Elliot Blass's (1991) advice.

APPLYING FOR A POSITION

As I decry indiscriminately applying for every advertised opening, choose carefully among those you will apply for. Not to care about the nature of an opening or about your suitability, in my opinion, shows a lack of purpose and discrimination. By electing to apply for only certain openings, you focus your efforts and those of the professors who write your letters of recommendation. A letter that covers all possibilities in the end covers none well and, worse yet, is so perceived by search committees.

Your first task is to prepare a curriculum vitae (CV). Today the composing of CVs (or résumés) seems to be a popular occupation (to judge from the inviting ads of copying services), and good advice abounds in the literature (Darley & Zanna, 1987; Hayes & Hayes, 1989; Wilbur, 1988) and the campus office of career planning. The CV should start with a section on personal information and, depending on the times and your own inclinations, may include your birth date, marital status, and number of children. Next, as part of your educational history, include any honors and the titles and advisors of your master's thesis and doctoral dissertation. Before you detail your professional experiences, name any other honors and awards and the professional societies to which you belong. (Recall that I urged you to apply for student membership in the important society or societies in your field.) Under the heading of professional experience, list any professional positions held and any courses taught. Here, it is appropriate to go into a bit of detail about what you actually did in each position, the titles of the courses taught, the degree of responsibility you carried for each, together with the student evaluations (which I hope were favorable). Next, list papers delivered at professional and scholarly meetings, by title, meeting, date, and place, and then articles published, by title, date, and journal. Be sure to include the names of your coauthors and, if you were one of two or more authors, to state the exact nature of your contribution.

Last come the names of the professors who will write letters for you. It goes without saying that you will have obtained their assent. To refresh their memories, give them a copy of your CV, a transcript of your courses and grades, and a description of the opening for which you are applying. Assuming that you have already discussed the openings with them, they can now compose a letter of recommendation that speaks exactly to your abilities in relation to the particular position or positions.

The cover letter you send with the CV, in my opinion, is as important as any part of your credentials. Nothing makes me want to place an applicant's folder in the reject pile faster than a form letter saying only, "I am submitting my CV for the opening in your department." In well-crafted sentences, provide some details about your research interests and teaching experiences, other professional experiences and special competencies, and your eventual goals. Many of these items will be listed in your CV, and some may seem too minor to be listed there, but in a cover letter it is proper to refer to a certain research experience or conference attended that had special meaning for you, and the insight you gained. Be informative but honest, and above all, be modest. Your readers have at one time written just such letters themselves and, furthermore, will read a great many like yours. Know, then, that they are shrewd and experienced, sensitive to exaggeration and self-congratulation.

PREPARING FOR THE INTERVIEW

Let us now proceed to the time when you receive an invitation for an interview. Fortunately, whatever anxiety the invitation generates will be dispelled by the work of preparing for the interview.

Your first task is to compose a talk for an audience of professors *and* students, and that is not easy: You need to impress the professors with your erudition and at the same time show that you can explain matters simply and lucidly. Generally, the talk will be based on your doctoral research and given in the usual form of papers presented at conventions, unfortunately a bit stiff and data-bound. To prepare it, get your data in good form, sharpen the phrasing of the questions, and show how the data provided answers. Inasmuch as most students speak poorly, heed the advice that lies everywhere at hand (recall that I advised you not to scoff at taking a course in speaking). Polish, memorize, and rehearse. Your talk will show how seriously you take the occasion, how organized you are, how efficiently you designed the study, how deep is your understanding of its significance, how clearly you present information, and how respectfully and cogently you respond to questions.

As another part of your preparation, learn as much as you can about the institution, the department, and the professors by studying catalogs and brochures, which you should request when you receive the invitation. What is the institution's history and philosophy of education, and what does it see as its mission? Consult the *Directory of the American Psychological Association* and others in your field, as well as relevant issues of *Who's Who*, to learn where the professors received their training and experience. Make time to read or reread their major publications. Be as interested in the professors as they will be in you; nothing bespeaks your interest in the position better than the evidence you give of knowing the work and theoretical orientation of your possible future colleagues. At the least, your interest in them is a mark of common courtesy.

THE INTERVIEW

Now to the visit. You will be interviewed by many persons: professors, the head of the department, some students, and possibly the dean, the provost, or the president—each differing in style, each judging you by a different set of criteria and expectations. Put your thoughts in order so that you can answer questions about your views of education, current trends in your discipline, and even about social policy and political affairs. You in turn will ask about the nature and number of courses you would be expected to teach; the size of classes and the system of grading; possibilities for research, including availability of subjects, space, equipment, computer facilities, and financial support; the tenure review policies; and sabbatical or other types of leaves for study and research. Another set of questions relates to housing, opportunities for your spouse if you are married, and the availability of day-care and the nature of schools if you have children. I have left the salary to the last and I trust you will not ask about it too early; many other characteristics of a position are more important, and salaries are much the same among similar institutions within a geographical area. When you do learn the salary, it is fitting to ask about fringe benefits.

Plan your visit so that you have some free time to sense the ambience of the setting. Walk the campus, visit the library and the student bookstore, wander through the students' shopping streets. Perchance someone will offer to drive you through parts of the town—more appropriate if the setting is not a large city. Obtain a college and a local newspaper to read on the way home. Ask yourself if this would be a congenial place for you and your family to live, study, and work. If it is, I hope you will receive an offer.

Be prepared for a period of waiting, seemingly interminable. Search committees interview other candidates, meet, debate, and consult other professors. Their decision is brought before the department's head and personnel committee for discussion and approval. The department's decision must then be approved by several administrative officers, including the dean, the provost, and the chancellor or president, and finally by the board of trustees. During all this time you wait in uncertainty.

SOME TYPES OF OPENINGS

A postdoctoral fellowship provides the opportunity to hone your research skills or to acquire a new area of competence in an academic, research, or clinical setting. Inquire closely about what is expected of you. Are you to take or audit courses? Are you to teach, and, if so, what? Are you to collaborate in the sponsor's research, and to what extent? How much time will you have to conduct your own research and to write papers? What is the sponsor's standing in the field, and how close is the fit between the sponsor's interests and your own? A postdoctoral fellowship maintains you in the familiar student role and postpones (but only temporarily) the search for a position. At its termination, however, you may well be in a more favored situation. You will have enriched your knowledge and perfected certain skills. You will likely have completed a study or two, given a paper at meetings, and submitted your dissertation to a journal. In the end, the greatest gain may be that you now have a firmer idea of the next position you want and of the area of your future research.

A position in a research institute, another possibility, offers the attractive opportunity to concentrate all your efforts on research and to join a group of colleagues similarly dedicated. Research institutes and centers are formed to solve problems that require the concerted efforts of a number of investigators from different disciplines. Sometimes university-based, they also often collaborate with industries and state governments. Furthermore, they provide many supporting services—statistical, computing, technical, and secretarial—that consume much of the time and energy of those who initiate their own research in a college or university. In general, also, you have no classes to teach (although you may elect to teach), no students to demand your time, no responsibility for collegiate self-government, and, early on, no need to find financial support. Yet, without students you sacrifice the larger view of the discipline that comes from teaching. And in a year or two, you may be expected to contribute to the writing of proposals for support. Ask yourself, before you apply, whether the research fires your enthusiasm and whether the director and other investigators command your respect. Then find out the exact nature of your duties and the degree of independence allowed. (See Redd [Supplement 2] in chapter 7 in this volume.)

For positions in institutions of higher learning, Gleckner (1988) provides a lively taxonomy of colleges and universities, based in part on his own experiences with several small and large, public and private institutions, in different parts of the country. He started as an instructor at the University of Wisconsin and at the time of writing was professor of English and director of graduate studies at Duke University. I commend his chapter to your attention.

In a 4-year liberal arts college, teaching is generally more important than research. In fact, some colleges grant tenure and promotion primarily on the basis of successful teaching. Yet all expect you to engage in research, recognizing that it can inform and enliven teaching. Moreover, a professor's research activities provide an arena in which undergraduates can obtain training and experience, necessary for their senior projects and almost a sine qua non for entry into graduate school. Furthermore, teaching in a liberal arts college entails more than meeting classes: It includes close advising and concern for the academic progress of each student. Given the smaller faculty, you carry responsibility not only for your own discipline but in equal measure for the governing of the college. And, at colleges in smaller communities, professors often find themselves becoming active in community affairs. Being more visible, they are called on to talk to parent–teacher associations and civic clubs and to serve on boards of social agencies. You may be a person who is attracted by the prospect of that richer participation in the life of a community.

At Rockford College I found still other sources of satisfaction. As the only professor of psychology (actually, an assistant professor because I did not yet have a PhD), I had to teach the different courses required for a major and thereby expanded my knowledge of current developments in areas beyond my previous concentration on clinical skills. Then, by teaching many of the same students in different courses, I was able to follow their progress and, given the small classes, to focus my efforts on ways to facilitate their development, both rewarding experiences for a psychologist. I profited also by coming to know professors of other disciplines and by seeing the world through their eyes, experiences not so easily gained in a large university.

A faculty position in a university you know from observing the activities of your professors. It requires teaching, research, and service to the university and the larger community. Research is highly valued, and you can teach graduate students. As in a liberal arts college, you enjoy the benefits and carry the responsibilities of academic freedom and enter into the condition of employment known as the tenure-track system. I scant a more complete description here because the life of a university professor is so fully portrayed throughout this book.

At the end, I group together a number of nontenured positions. Some, like that of instructor, are expected to lead, after some three yearly reappointments, to promotion to the rank of assistant professor. Others are designated as visiting or fixed 1-year appointments (such as adjunct, clinical, or research) that may carry no or only a limited commitment for further employment. To these must be added part-time teaching or research appointments. Decisions among these possibilities are some of the most difficult. But any position may be better than none, and, if you give each your best, it may develop into something more attractive, possibly even a full-time tenured position. As Gleckner (1988) said, "You may not find a new Jerusalem in your first job, but after all, you all know what was not built in a day" (p. 18).

This account covers only some of the more common types of positions. Persons interested in social policy often serve as American Association for the Advancement of Science (AAAS) Congressional Fellows, as advisors to child and family advocacy organizations, or as consultants to state and federal agencies.

I trust that in this section I have not glossed too lightly over the many uncertainties in one of the more difficult periods of your early professional life. Not only must you choose among the possible openings, but all the time you are aware of the many persons competing for them and are uncertain of how you compare. Even the offer of a position can cause an agony of indecision. Take your time, consult your mentors, and rest assured that no position closes doors to your future. You will learn from each, and each can open the door to another.

II

THE YEARS OF ARRIVING

3

BEING A MEMBER OF A FACULTY

The first day of classes is fast approaching and you have several urgent concerns. Where does your first class meet? Have the textbooks arrived? When will you see your first paycheck? Urgent as these concerns are, I brush them aside. They are but the stuff of everyday life; they will be solved sooner or later and will fade away. Instead, I ask you to contemplate a matter of deep philosophical import that will sustain you as you continue to meet one after another of these concerns: I ask you to consider what it means to be a member of a faculty.

Well may you wonder at my beginning a chapter that purports to introduce you to your chosen profession by bringing up a matter that is more often taken for granted than examined. But to be a member of a faculty means more than teaching students what you have learned; it means joining a community of teachers bound by common interests and engaged in a common pursuit, a community with an ancient and distinguished past and with a present both demanding and promising. Do I exaggerate? Let us wait until the end of the chapter to judge.

THE RIGHT OF ACADEMIC FREEDOM

A faculty member is first and foremost a teacher and a scholar. As such, you enjoy academic freedom, an esteemed privilege long zealously defended (Fellman, 1973; Hofstadter & Metzger, 1955; Morrow, 1968). By this right you are free to study, to inquire, to speak your mind, and to assert the truth as you see it, without fear of dismissal.

The right of academic freedom was codified in the 1940 Statement of Principles on Academic Freedom and Tenure by the American Association of University Professors (AAUP, 1990b). Endorsed since then by scores of professional and educational organizations, the statement is honored and protected by institutions of higher learning across the country, any limitations being clearly stated by a particular institution. You are granted the right not for your personal benefit or that of your institution, but for the common good, which depends on the free search for truth. And you are granted that right only because of your ability and training and the promise of continued progress.

The principle of tenure, a correlative part of the 1940 statement, ensures academic freedom by providing the economic security to make the profession attractive to men and women of ability. But even during the probationary period before tenure is granted—that is, from the first day of your appointment—you have the same right of academic freedom as all members of the faculty.

So great a right entails many obligations—to your discipline, to your institution, to society, and above all, to your students. Just as you are free to study, inquire, and speak your mind, you must see that your students have the same freedoms. Guide them and counsel them. Be fair, patient, generous, and sympathetic. Put them first in your appointment book and at the head of your responsibilities. The freedom of the professor to teach is but one side of the coin of academic freedom; the other side is the freedom of the student to learn.

As zealously as faculty members guard their right to academic freedom, so do they guard their responsibility for academic matters on the campus. Although institutions of higher learning are legally controlled by governing boards, the faculty members determine who attends, what they study, and how they are examined. The faculty also determine who deserves to join their ranks and when the newcomers will be promoted and granted tenure. You can begin now to anticipate the increasing influence you will have, beyond the lecture you give, the research you conduct, or the paper you write, in setting academic standards and values. For now, see in collegial government a source of pride in what it means to be a member of a faculty.

You are, of course, also a citizen. Although as a citizen you are free to speak your mind, as a member of a faculty and a representative of an institution of higher learning you are expected to be accurate, modest and not overbearing, respectful and not arrogant, and to make clear that you are speaking not for the institution but for yourself.

These rights and responsibilities define your place as a member of a faculty. The importance of your discipline recedes for the moment as you acquire a sense of that place: a member of a faculty of a particular institution with a history, situated in a certain part of the country, and nourished by its own distinctive cultural and intellectual traditions.

Your rights and responsibilities are spelled out in the faculty code of your school. Were there any limitations of academic freedom because of religious or other aims of the institution, you would have known and agreed to them when you took the position. The space I have devoted to this topic shows how much I value academic freedom and its obligations, but even as I urge you to study your institution's code, I have to report that neither I nor the professors I canvassed on my corridor could find in our offices the latest issue of our own institution's code. May I assume that nevertheless all of us were thoroughly informed?

In summary, the right of academic freedom, although apparently simple, proves on reflection to be complex. It gives you as a member of a faculty the right to teach your discipline and to add to knowledge, but that right is hedged: You are granted that right because it is deemed to be in society's interest and because you have worked to acquire the ability to do so. Then, you are not only the custodian of your students' right to think and study unhampered, but you are also their wise and concerned mentor. To ensure these rights, you, in fellowship with your colleagues, take responsibility for the academic standards of your institution. Finally, you are not only a teacher and a member of an institution of higher learning but also a citizen constrained by behavior befitting your station in life.

Think of these rights and responsibilities when you run into difficulties. They will strengthen your hand and fill you with wonder and pride and humility. (See also Freedman [Supplement 1] in chapter 7 in this volume.) Now let us turn to the day-to-day activities to honor your rights and fulfill your obligations.

ESTABLISHING COLLEGIAL RELATIONS

As a new member of a faculty, you can count on a warm reception. Appreciate it and meet it in like spirit. Show an interest in the work of your colleagues, in their research or special projects, and read their papers. Spend time in your office and on campus, join your colleagues for lunch, and do not hesitate to seek their help when problems arise. Yet, withal, you have to function as an independent person, not expecting to find among your colleagues the same kind of assistance you received from professors when you were a student.

Be circumspect in joining alliances prematurely, and if, unfortunately, you sense factions or cliques, steer clear of them. Nothing is more wasteful of time and destructive of work and inner harmony than to become a party to gossip, to detailing hurts and resentments. I know—easier said than done. Still, in the face of dissension, be polite, distant, preoccupied, and turn your attention to your work.

As a member of the faculty, you of course will participate in the affairs of your department; they include advising students, serving on senior, honors, master's, and doctoral committees, attending colloquia, transporting and entertaining visitors, attending faculty meetings, and reading papers for colleagues. Furthermore, keep the head of your department informed of your plans for teaching and research, the students you are advising, the community and other services you are performing, and any problems you are encountering. In time, you may be asked to work with the colloquium committee, to review requests for the library, to participate in the setting of ethical standards for research with human participants, or to serve as the department liaison with various honorary societies. Departments generally are sensitive to your needs during the first year or two, and you will not be burdened early. Accept such assignments cheerfully and turn in a sterling performance, but do not accept so many that they interfere with your teaching and other scholarly pursuits. You would not be happy when the day came for you to be considered for tenure if the personnel committee faced the quandary of how to give credit for much committee work in a record lacking in effective teaching or original research and scholarship.

Early on, learn the administrative procedures of your institution. To govern itself, every institution has a set of rules about the attendance of students, the grading of their performance, the courses in which final examinations must be given and the times thereof, the periods in which no quizzes or papers may be assigned, and so on. These rules, the result of continuing deliberation by faculty councils and administration, are not to be taken lightly. Although the principle of academic freedom applies to what you teach and study, it does not offer license to make your own regulations. At the same time, learn your responsibilities for upholding the honor code and the campus code governing academic work. On my campus, faculty council legislation stipulates that "Academic work is a joint enterprise involving faculty and students. Both have a fundamental responsibility for ensuring its integrity." Abide by the regulations and do not write your own in defiance of them.

ADVISING STUDENTS

Serving your students as an intellectual guide and counselor, an obligation attendant on your right of academic freedom, I translate into being an advisor. Some students may ask for no more than approval of their course schedules; others may seek your advice on a host of concerns, including plans and hopes for their future. Much advising, of course, takes place in the context of your teaching—providing help as needed, and inspiration as appropriate. For needs that go beyond your competence, learn the sources of assistance on your campus, such as the office of the dean, the centers for tutoring, counseling, and financial aid, and the health services. Be responsive, encouraging, and sympathetic. Be sensitive enough not to intrude on those who seem not to welcome advice, yet concerned enough to offer it to those who could profit by attention. Long after students leave the campus many will cherish your interest even as you yourself now recall the professors who showed such an interest in you and your progress.

Being asked by students to serve on their senior, honors, master's, or doctoral committee is an honor, and to serve as an advisor, an even greater honor. You are asked because they think you will be interested in the topic and can contribute to it. Take the invitation seriously, study the proposal, review the student's record of courses and grades, and confer with the student's advisor. Be prepared for hours of work. Your acceptance of the invitation, therefore, should be a matter of considered deliberation. As for a student's electing you as an advisor, acceptance is even more serious. This academic relationship is one of the most important in your personal and professional life. You will find yourself spending almost as much time on your student's research as on your own. Your efforts constitute the legacy you confer in terms of your ethical and scientific values, and the student constitutes your legacy to the future.

Be especially circumspect in accepting a student who was previously the advisee of another professor. Be mindful of that professor's feelings, because, in general, no one likes to lose a student to another (although sometimes the professor is relieved). Proceed cautiously, and accept the student only with the first professor's approval. But if you have students who wish to change to other advisors, release them promptly and gracefully.

VALUING YOUR HELPERS

Throughout your career, many persons besides your colleagues help you: secretaries, teaching and research assistants, work-study students, and undergraduates who contribute to your research. These individuals play a very important part in your career—however small their services may seem when taken for granted—and the best avenue to appreciating them is to imagine life without them. If you share a secretary's time with other faculty members, realize that your priorities may not be the same as theirs. Find out how much "lead time" is required to complete the work you submit, and rarely, if ever, ask that your work be placed ahead of that of others.

With your other helpers, lean over backwards not to exploit them, and do acknowledge their help whenever you can. Very soon they become individuals for whose careers and welfare you feel responsible. For those letters of recommendation they are sure to request in the future, keep track now of the tasks they perform and of their special abilities. Remember that you, too, were once in their position; now it is your turn to treat them honorably and generously.

JOINING A COMMUNITY OF SCHOLARS

Now that you are a faculty member, don't forget to change from student to member status in your professional societies. Unfortunately, the cost is considerable. Still, membership signifies commitment to your profession and discipline and provides information about meetings, the call for papers, and in many cases, the journals you need to keep informed. And, if you can afford the time and money, celebrate your new status by now attending the meetings as a member of a faculty.

One more new honor is yours: joining your colleagues in academic dress at commencement. The history of academic dress reaches far back into the early days of the oldest universities. A statute of 1321 required that all "Doctors, Licentiates, and Bachelors" of the University of Coimbra in Portugal wear gowns. For centuries such gowns were worn by students and faculty even as they attended classes, and as late as 1927 Professor Edward Bradford Titchener lectured in his academic gown during the first course I took in psychology at Cornell University. Reserved today for formal occasions, the gowns and hoods, their colors, trimmings, and patterns spell each wearer's degree and field of learning as well as the college or university conferring the degree.

The faculty's participation in commencement is prescribed, but in larger institutions it is often disregarded, especially if one's absence is not conspicuous. Many younger professors, not yet fully conscious of the fellowship of scholars, disdain participating; to march in a procession accoutered in a quaint costume harking back to medieval times can indeed be viewed today as pompous, ostentatious, and irrelevant. In another view, however, the procession of the faculty affirms a scholarly tradition and signifies the faculty's allegiance to the aims of higher education as well as to their discipline and the institution from which they graduated. For the students and their parents, the procession affirms the role of the faculty in providing the education on which the students' graduation is based.

How truly the academic procession symbolizes the community of scholars impressed me most vividly at the inauguration in 1986 of C. Dixon Spangler as the new president of my university. For such ceremonies, the presidents of other colleges and universities are invited. If they cannot attend, they send representatives, usually alumni who live at no great distance. Thus was I honored to represent Hanna Holborn Gray, president of the University of Chicago. I experienced a great uplift of spirit when I marched in academic regalia with 105 other presidents and delegates, ordered by year of their institution's founding—beginning with the University of Paris (12th century)—as well as with delegates from the learned societies. At that moment I sensed the meaning of a community of scholars, a community extending beyond my campus and beyond that moment of time to the far reaches of the world and back through the centuries.

For these many reasons, I urge you to participate in faculty processions. You will find the experience rewarding. True, academic regalia is expensive. Although it can be rented fairly reasonably, purchase it as early as you can to reduce the cost of each wearing. By the way, at the head of your list of desired graduation gifts, the wish for academic regalia may fall on receptive ears.

CODA

And now I take you back to the beginning of this chapter. I have told you more than you want to know, and right now you do not have the time to give these matters their due. Indeed, years may pass before any of us comprehends the full meaning of academic freedom, but if on the eve of a demanding position you take a little time to reflect on the matter, it will help you shed the persona of a graduate student and assume that of a professor.

So, when the going gets rough, when you stumble, when you wonder if you have chosen the right profession, turn to the beginning of this chapter and read it again. There you will find the inspiration to sustain you. Judge now whether I exaggerated.

4

THE ENTERPRISE OF TEACHING

To teach is a privilege and an honor: a privilege, because you are given the opportunity to tell others what you know; and an honor, because in the opinion of some responsible persons you were judged able to do so. As you face a class, however, the privilege and the honor may seem remote indeed.

So highly is research valued during graduate training that the importance of teaching is often scanted. Yet in any academic position, whether in a research university or a liberal arts college, you are hired to teach, and therein lies your primary responsibility—to the students, to the institution, to society, and no less, to your discipline. Moreover, teaching profits the teacher; as William B. Aycock, professor of law at the University of North Carolina (UNC) at Chapel Hill, said on the occasion of his retirement in 1985 (Silva, 1985), "Teaching is the core of learning, but you have to do a lot of learning to do a little teaching."

At its simplest level, teaching concentrates your attention and structures your day. Too often our thoughts churn unfocused; too often our energy is dissipated to no effect. But the effort required to communicate what you know—simply, concisely, and effectively—hones and focuses your own knowledge. Often, as you hear yourself speak, it dawns on you that there is no established, or only very shaky, evidence for what you are saying. Or, a question from a student shocks you into awareness of your inability to answer: you do not know the answer, or even the evidence on which to base an answer. Such events send you back to the books or into the laboratory; either way, you gain. Teaching a class, furthermore, provides a sense of accomplishment, whereas a day spent endlessly rewriting that opening paragraph to a scholarly paper often does not. Of what other endeavors can you say as much for any one hour of your day? As Henry Gleitman (1984) vividly stated the matter, "I can say to myself on any day: My experiments are going badly; I just lost my research grant; a paper of mine was rejected; my daughter has measles; and I had an argument with my wife. But—I gave a great Psych 1 lecture, and so all is well" (p. 427).

For all these reasons, welcome the opportunity to teach, and come to enjoy it. Know, too, that as I write, national concerns about the quality of teaching are rising, especially the teaching of undergraduates at large universities where the faculty's research efforts are thought to garner greater rewards than do their teaching efforts. Teaching continues to be esteemed highly enough for the APA to designate one of its earliest divisions (Division 2) as the Teaching of Psychology, composed of psychologists for whom teaching is of prime importance. Membership in the Division includes a subscription to its journal, The Teaching of Psychology, described as the "leading source of information and inspiration for all who teach psychology." At national and regional meetings, the Division sponsors papers, symposia, and workshops that provide a forum for innovation in courses and teaching. Furthermore, each issue of the Monitor devotes a section to teaching, and the American Psychological Foundation yearly presents a Distinguished Teaching Award (which Henry Gleitman received in 1983).

THE CRAFT OF TEACHING

To teach is a skill to be learned, to be practiced, and ever to be perfected. It is a skill not automatically guaranteed by knowledge of your subject matter, for that by itself will not stimulate students. Good teachers are not abashed to report their continuing efforts to perfect their technique (e.g., Angell, 1936; Gleitman, 1984). Fortunately, aids to improving your teaching abound. Books and articles range from the inspirational to the practical. Joseph Epstein (1981) observed that "What all the great teachers appear to have in common is love of their subject, an obvious satisfaction in arousing this love in their students, and an ability to convince them that what they are being taught is deadly serious" (p. xii). On the practical side, you will learn from McKeachie (1986) that you should begin preparing for any course 3 months before it starts; from Lowman (1984) you will learn how to remember the names of even a large class of students; and from all of them you will learn much, much more.

Avail yourself also of the services of any office on your campus dedicated to improving teaching skills. Such teaching and learning (or faculty improvement) centers offer workshops for teaching assistants and young professors, as well as advice for professors at any level on how to revise a course or develop a new one.

Good practice recommends giving the students a syllabus for each course you teach. It should list the course objectives, the texts to be used, the required readings, other assignments with due dates, and the nature and schedule of examinations. In the syllabus, and certainly at the first class meeting, you should remind students of their responsibility to uphold your school's honor code governing academic performance, of what constitutes plagiarism, and of what you consider inappropriate assistance for assignments and examinations. The administrative guidelines of my own department caution that giving a few minutes to these matters early on may save you a great deal of unpleasantness later. In fact, our chancellor encourages the faculty not only to include a statement about the school's honor code in their syllabi but also to read it aloud at the first meeting of a class. I find particularly impressive the opening paragraph of the directive: "Academic dishonesty in any form is unacceptable, because any breach in academic integrity, however small, strikes destructively at the University's life and work."

Beyond the specific objectives for different courses, the general objectives for all courses should consider how each question evolved, how scientists proceed to obtain answers to these questions, and how in the answering they observe the ethical standards governing research with human and animal subjects. The topic of ethical standards invariably interests students and you can count on it to evoke a lively discussion.

TEACHING MATERIALS

From the many possible textbooks, choose the one that comes closest to your own theoretical views; otherwise you will be refuting the author at every point. (However, to increase my own knowledge and to provide variety, I chose a different text every semester that I taught introductory psychology at Rockford College.) Unless a text systematically builds each concept on the previous one, the ordering of its chapters need not be your ordering. Further, the usual early chapters that justify the importance of the subject matter, replete with definitions and theories, can make dull reading for the uninitiated. Instead, break with tradition and start with a topic of wide interest: one not yet resolved, and one about which opposing points of view offer controversies worth pondering. For example, in introductory psychology, "intelligence" could be that topic: What is it? How is it measured? What factors contribute to its definition? What is its role in everyday life? What are its implications for educational and social policy?

The topic "nature and nurture" offers a similarly provocative introduction to many psychology courses.

In the end, textbooks are at best secondhand presentations of the original thinking and research of others—restless thought distilled into static outlines. If your students are to learn how problems evolved and developed, if they are to gain insight into inquiring minds at work, consider assigning at least a few classic papers by the past masters, all of whom wrote simply, clearly, and vigorously. Selected papers by Darwin, Freud, William James, and Skinner, among others, will give them contact with the thinking that has nourished many of us.

Similarly, in every course students will profit by studying a few journal articles to gain firsthand knowledge of psychological research in the making. If you assign articles you yourself have authored, or reports of studies in which participated, you can then explain how the research question arose and how you decided to answer it—including choice of subjects, variables to measure, how the data were reduced and tested, the painstaking efforts at control, the false starts and revisions, the constrained nature of conclusions and speculation, and above all, the ethical principles governing the use of subjects, whether human or nonhuman. Journal articles inform students about the questioning nature of research; they can serve as models for their senior or honors projects; and most importantly, they provide guidelines for evaluating research findings not only now, but for the rest of their lives.

Valuable indeed would be a chance for students in every course in psychology to carry out small research projects—always, of course, in full compliance with the ethical principles governing research. They would then profit by experiencing "a taste of participating in the expansion of scholarship rather than merely receiving the results of such expansion" (Pelikan, 1983, p. 38). Many handbooks offer a variety of classroom demonstrations and exercises that provide similar opportunities (e.g., the three volumes of *Activities Handbook for the Teaching of Psychology*, published by the APA [Benjamin & Lowman, 1981; Makosky, Sileo, Whittemore, Landry, & Skutley, 1990; Makosky, Whittemore, & Rogers, 1988]).

Films and audiotapes extend the range of teaching materials, as do videotapes of your own or other professors' work in progress, and the daily newspapers speak to every facet of behavior. I am recommending variety, not for its own sake, but to show the students the abundance of riches in our discipline and how it lights up the far reaches of all that goes into the study of behavior.

Today you can combine some of these materials in a "course pack" of your own design, including sections from different textbooks, chapters from edited books, readings from those seminal thinkers, and selected journal articles. The student is freed from looking for and sometimes not finding the material in the library or the computer; copy centers relieve you of worries about infringing copyright laws; and you gain the pleasure of teaching from your "own" book.

CLASSROOM TEACHING

A teacher teaches students and not the course of study listed in the catalog. If we so regard the enterprise of teaching, I propose that we are on our way to fulfilling our proper role. But we have one more precept to guide our behavior: that we present ourselves not as all-knowing but, to paraphrase Alfred North Whitehead (1929/1957), in our "true character" as ignorant persons thinking, actively utilizing our small share of knowledge (p. 58).

To enlist the students as partners you can encourage them to regard every sentence you utter not as an assertion but as a question. Thus, you can ask "How do we know this? What is the evidence? Is some other explanation possible?"—and wait for a response from the class before you try to frame the answer. J. R. Angell (1936) reported in his autobiography that he gave many hours to perfecting a Socratic technique of questioning. His aim was "to learn so to phrase lucid questions that they will provoke significant thinking and when answered will open up the next directly related issue and so make the entire class hour one of active thought for every student . . ." (p. 11). "Active thought" seems to me an apt phrase for what a teacher is trying to accomplish.

Your classroom teaching will be much improved when you can wean yourself from a scripted text to a one-page outline of the topic for the day. All of us can feel for the inexperienced (perhaps out of our own first attempts) who go to class with pages of carefully gathered and organized notes, confident that they have enough material to last the 50 minutes— only to find that they have worked their way through the material in 30 minutes and now face 20 minutes of stunned speechlessness. In contrast, with only that one page of notes, you are freed to think on your feet. You will talk to the students and watch them so that you can repeat, paraphrase, or expand in response to their puzzled expressions. You can pause as you search for a word, and even utter an ill-formed sentence in the process of offering your thoughts not as *made* but as *being* made. Although you can read your notes without thinking, to talk, you must think.

If you must, write out the lecture, but leave all those pages in your office. In reviewing Vladimir Nabokov's published lectures with their many new notes on old margins, V. S. Pritchett (1981), himself a professor, said Nabokov knew that "a spotless text is death to the lecturer." In fact, you might do well to file that script and those pages of notes in a bottom drawer. New facts and new ideas appear in every journal, and each forces you to reexamine what you know. "Were we to teach yesterday's knowledge today, the quickening rate of its obsolescence would betray our students tomorrow" (Kasarda, 1985, p. 3). Thus, as we read and write, teach, and conduct research, we are continually reorganizing what we think we know. When you bring these revisions in your own understanding to the students' attention, they observe that in the process of teaching, you, too, are in the process of learning (see Josh Haskett's letter [Supplement 1] at the end of this chapter).

I cannot end this section without acknowledging the stage fright and nightmares that beset many teachers. I myself recall such extreme nervousness upon facing the first meeting of a class (about 1934) that, to calm myself as the students filed in, I wrote the word "psychology" over and over, until after some twenty attempts it began to become legible. Even today, I experience a measure of stage fright for the first few meetings of even a small class. Fortunately, the agitation dissipates as one begins to talk. And, in nightmares the night before a class meeting, you may find yourself without notes, in the wrong room, or incompletely dressed. Then, at odd moments during the day and as you fall asleep, you will often find yourself framing sentences and questions to make a point in your next lecture—so compellingly does teaching occupy the mind of the teacher.

TESTING STUDENTS

Tests should not be regarded as instruments of punishment for students, nor as portents of unpopularity for the teacher, but rather as effective tools to foster learning and improve teaching. They can play an important role in teaching, but not if they are restricted to the prescribed midterm and final examinations. Instead, frequent tests keep students working throughout the course; at the same time, they inform them of your standards and you of your success in teaching.

Such tests as I have in mind, being short, may more appropriately be termed quizzes, and can take many forms (but not of the multiple-choice type). The simplest may ask, at the end of a class meeting, for a brief summary of the main topic just presented or for a statement of why it is important. Short-answer tests, limited to a few paragraphs, can ask the students to solve a problem, propose a hypothesis about the information just presented, or suggest implications for practice or social policy. Short essays—two or three pages on some thought-provoking question related to the current topic—may be assigned for completion outside of class. Still another alternative may ask that the first and last paragraphs of an essay be written and the body only outlined. The students will be grateful if you tell them that the first couple of assignments will not be graded, but that you will return them with comments, and any may be rewritten.

In decrying the use of true–false and multiple-choice questions, I am defending the value of writing as a creative process that demands hard thinking and close reasoning. As a result of your comments and suggestions, you will be pleased to see that your students' papers improve miraculously. Unaccustomed though they may be to such demands in a *science* course, most students do know how to write.

When grading written papers, try to treat the answers as though you yourself were the writer—that is, gently and with respect. Appreciate what the students are trying to say, and word your comments and corrections so thoughtfully that they will be grateful for your efforts—a tall order, indeed, but true to the role of a teacher. Then, because assigning grades to essay questions is more subjective than counting the number of correct answers to true–false or multiple-choice questions, spend some class time discussing your standards. Describe the characteristics of the good answer, the average answer, and the poor answer. Talk of the importance you attach to accuracy, the ability to weigh evidence, and originality. Certainly, to evaluate and comment on even short answers and essays demands time and energy, especially as the papers should be returned promptly. (You will lighten the burden as you learn to frame the assignments ever more precisely.) The effort is small, however, compared to the learning it fosters and the teaching it enhances; indeed, for me it defines "quality" teaching.

THE CASE FOR STUDENT EVALUATIONS

Although student evaluations can be challenged on many grounds (including the appropriateness of their use as measures of a teacher's effectiveness in matters of promotion, tenure, and salary), they nevertheless can provide you with useful information. Therefore, why restrict them to the last day of the class (or worse yet, to the final examination)? Rather, you can design your own evaluations to assess how well your classroom activities and assignments are meeting your objectives for that course. Administer them early in the course and once or twice more. They should be filled out anonymously, perhaps taken home overnight to allow for reflection, and later discussed in class. See them as an instrument to help you realize your goals and to give the students a voice in their own education. I agree with Kenneth Eble (1983), who said that "faculty members interested in learning about their teaching cut off a vital source of information if . . . they are hostile or indifferent to student evaluations" (p. 137). Let us trust the students to grade us as intelligently as we grade them.

TEACHING GRADUATE STUDENTS

Courses in graduate school prepare students for a professional life devoted to scholarship, inquiry, and service as teachers, researchers, and contributors to human welfare. Here the professor's task is to teach them to evaluate what is known and to discover what more needs to be known. That task, in my opinion, is often better accomplished when the class is led by the professor than by the students, although many combinations fall between these extremes.

To support my opinion, I cite two very different examples from my own experience in graduate courses (these examples also speak to the relative merits of formal lectures and unstructured discussions). In a course in anthropology at the University of Chicago, Robert Redfield began his lectures in session after session by asking himself provocative questions, such as "What characterizes a society as primitive?" He then proceeded to answer the question by weighing the evidence for each possible characteristic until he had arrived at an answer. To hear such a first-rate mind thinking aloud was a memorable experience; if classroom discussion ensued, I don't remember it. In another class, taught by Carl Rogers, at each meeting students in turn read papers on topics of their choice (required to be submitted in writing before the first meeting); the papers were then discussed by the students and Dr. Rogers, who was as nondirective in teaching as he was in therapy. That I found this experience unsatisfying probably reveals as much about me as about the class—but what I am trying to say is that lectures need not be deadening and that student-led classes are not always inspiring.

In teaching developmental psychology (aside from lectures and a great deal of focused discussion), I favored assigning the writing of short essays, restricted to five pages and a page of references, on topics demanding a creative use of knowledge. To that end, I gave the students extensive lists of readings in books, chapters, and journal articles, including references to many early and classical works. I judged their papers for their grasp of abstract concepts, precision in the use of terms, the marshalling and weighing of evidence, the use of primary rather than secondary sources and, of course, the clarity of the writing. I returned the papers promptly, with comments acknowledging good statements and challenging weaker ones. We discussed the papers in class, and I was pleased to find that together we reached an understanding of the topics that was both broader and deeper than any one of us, myself included, had held before. Parenthetically, I should note that the students knew that they could discuss their papers with me out-of-class and could rewrite any. In their course evaluations, the essays were often singled out for comment; some students complained about the amount of work or the difficulty of obtaining the references, but to my surprise, they and many others thanked me for my efforts to improve their writing and for their newly acquired familiarity with the library's resources.

TEACHING YOUR GRADUATE ADVISEES

As an advisor of graduate students, you enter into a special kind of relationship: that of a wise and trusted mentor. You have only a few years in which to teach them all you know so that they can turn in a handsome performance in whatever position they will assume after they leave you. Of the many charges you assume, the most obvious is leading them through their master's and doctoral research. Here you teach them how to formulate questions and how to devise methods for answering them. You assist them in acquiring subjects, space, and equipment; you closely supervise their gathering of data; and you introduce them to the services of statistical consultants. You also coach them on how to present their plans and findings to examining committees (see my Instructions to a Student [Supplement 2] at the end of this chapter) and supervise the writing of their final documents. Throughout the process, you encourage them to move beyond your own research questions, as you continue to instruct them in the ethical standards governing research and the use of subjects.

Your efforts on their behalf go far beyond even these weighty responsibilities. You help them plan their schedules and encourage them to move outside their discipline to take courses in mathematics, other sciences, and philosophy. You talk to them about the meaning of academic freedom and collegial self-government. You alert them to agencies that offer fellowships for training and subsidies to defray the costs of research and scholarly efforts. You prompt them to join professional and learned societies, to attend meetings and conferences, and to respond to calls for presentations. You watch over their teaching of undergraduates; refer them to guides, lectures, and workshops to improve their efforts; and review the student evaluations of their teaching. (See Guidelines by Meredith J. West [Supplement 3] at the end of this chapter.) You share your day-by-day professional duties with them and seek their advice as you prepare your own articles and grant applications. You miss no occasion to improve their speaking and writing. You bring position openings to their attention, help them define their goals, and are careful not to hold up a position similar to your own as the only way to justify your efforts on their behalf. You will certainly sympathize with their problems. And, of course, you will be available.

I set forth a tall order—but not too tall when you realize how important you are to your advisees and they to you. For them, you will forever be their mentor. Your words will follow them, and they will gauge their future behavior by the example you set. On the other hand, for you, these graduate students represent the embodiment of your standards and your ideals—they are your legacy to the future.

LAST WORDS

These pages spell out my conviction that teaching is as altruistic and important a profession as any. Teaching calls forth pride in the profession, humility in the wealth of knowledge, and concern for the minds of future generations. As we teach, we not only come to know more than we knew before, but we also become more than we were before. Through us, our students likewise not only know more than they knew before, but also become more than they were before. So it is that as teachers, we can never know for certain where our influence stops. Henry Adams (1931) may have been right in saying, "A teacher affects eternity" (p. 300).

SUPPLEMENT 1

EXCERPTS FROM A LETTER OF
A FORMER STUDENT

JOSH HASKETT

January 1972

Today was the last day of classes at the college. It was a very joyous occasion for me. . . . My special lecture series challenged the students beyond all my expectations; they began to write seriously and thoughtfully, speak up and talk among themselves as well as with me in our discussions. The classes became serious encounters where I could watch the students growing and where they could watch me growing too.

I learned . . . how great it is to discover that students are not just faces to talk *to*, but histories to draw upon and interact with, and change, and of course to learn from. And I learned an enormous amount. They pushed me as I pushed them. The fantastic thing, they have told me themselves, is that they actually *watched* me change, from the traditional lecturer, "role of teacher" type into someone more human, novel to them in their undergraduate world, into someone they were sorry they were going to leave in January. I had acquired positive properties!

And I guess I'm the only teacher of large classes who didn't use multiple-choice exams. It's been a real work load, of course. But most of the students have changed. Their first essays if they weren't simply copied were horrible. I'm going over their final essays now and the change is there! And the joy!

SUPPLEMENT 2

INSTRUCTIONS TO A STUDENT (HELEN R. ELNEKAVE) FOR PRESENTING A PROPOSAL AT A PREDOCTORAL ORAL EXAMINATION

HARRIET L. RHEINGOLD

March 1980

Be present in the assigned room at least 10 minutes ahead of time. It may be locked and you may need to locate the key. The room may have been left in an untidy state. Tidy it, straighten the chairs, and clean the blackboard. If you are using visual aids, check the equipment, and then once again.

Do not get so dressed up that you look unfamiliar. The proceedings are serious indeed but academic, and in Chapel Hill the mode of dress is informal.

After the examiners are assembled, I will ask you to leave the room. This procedure could be unsettling unless you know in advance that in your absence I will briefly sketch your academic performance and review the requirements for the examination (as specified by the University and the Department) that you have satisfied. I will ask if they have any questions about your progress, and then if they know any reasons why the examination should not proceed. When everyone is satisfied that you are ready to be examined, you are called back into the room.

You may assume that the examiners have read your proposal, but do not assume that they have every detail in mind. Do not be disturbed by some examiner's reading it while you are speaking, even if apparently for the first time.

Plan to take 10 minutes to present your proposal. Know what you

45

intend to say so well that you do not need to refer to your notes. In orderly fashion, tell what you plan to do and why. Do not review the literature, except as the work of others provides a thesis you seek to examine or a measure you intend to use. Begin with a simple statement of the proposal (e.g., to examine the effect of older siblings on children's behavior). Now present the ages of the children and defend the choices. Do not be too specific about the number of subjects because you should know enough to realize that it depends on the variability of the behaviors. Then present the plan for control and experimental groups, and what the control group will control for. How will these children be selected? Will you balance for sex, and so on? Next, present the procedure. Describe the experimental setting, directions to the participants, duration of trials and intertrial intervals.

The next part I consider the most difficult: defining the measures and defending them. Which theoretical considerations determined your choices? What information does each measure yield? How will that information contribute to the purpose of your study? Here you can refer to your own previous work and to the literature. At some point now you should tell how you will record the behaviors, code them, table them, and obtain observer agreement.

In the next section (and you should be almost—but not quite—at the end), summarize what you expect to find. For example, measures of these behaviors will provide information on so-and-so; measures of these other behaviors will provide information on this other class of behavior; and together they should provide information on the main effect you are studying. Can you build in a replication? Are you flexible enough to lump some of your measures to reduce their number? How would you lump and why? Or split?

The final section should reveal your awareness of embarking on a course of study that may not yield what you expect. Show that you understand the nature of research; that the results may suggest another and more telling study; and that you recognize that approval by the committee is not in the nature of a contract assuring you the degree.

Finally, know that any examiner has the right and even the duty to test your knowledge not only about your proposal but about psychology in general. It is here also that you may need to refer to the historical background of your proposal.

Be thoughtful, inquiring, modest. Be ready to weigh suggestions. Defend your plan but do not be defensive. And do not expect me to help you; I almost never do, although I will take notes for you. After the examiners seem to have concluded their questioning, I will ask you to leave the room. Do not be disturbed if we seem to take a long time. We may be only arguing among ourselves, or discussing the economy, or just chatting (it has happened).

Good luck! And get a good night's sleep.

SUPPLEMENT 3

GUIDELINES FOR SUPERVISING GRADUATE STUDENTS' TEACHING OF DEVELOPMENTAL PSYCHOLOGY

MEREDITH J. WEST

University of North Carolina at Chapel Hill

May 1980

Listed below are the informal guidelines I have used during the past 5 years in supervising graduate student teaching. It strikes me, in reviewing them, that the supervision consists of giving information and instruction, sharing knowledge and experiences, generally being available, and giving *prompt* feedback. The latter is absolutely essential. We cannot expect students to seek our help or follow our advice if they must stand in line for a week to get it. I have set aside office hours and made it clear that the students could call or ask for help or a free lecture at any time, and have offered 24-hour service on all questions about written assignments, grade decisions, and so on.

SELECTION OF TEXTBOOK AND READINGS

Before the semester begins, I make the books I have available for the students to consider, and I give my recommendations. In the past, I have tried to have all students teaching for the first time use the same book, to facilitate supervision and to allow me to evaluate exam questions and exam performance. I also make available past course outlines from previous students to help in deciding on course structure.

SUBMISSION OF COURSE OUTLINE AND PLANS
FOR ASSIGNMENTS

I require students to give me an outline of lecture topics and plans
for assignments, such as papers and research projects. I then meet with
them and make suggestions. I try to allow great freedom in lecture topics
but advise against spending the entire first month on theories, on a reca-
pitulation of Psychology 206–207 (graduate courses in Developmental), or
on a review in lecture form of that student's comprehensives. I often go
through my own course outline and explain the reasons for the topics and
sequence. On topics for papers or research projects, I usually spend some
time discussing those that I know work well or don't work well (e.g., giving
so much latitude that everybody ends up writing papers on autism); on
research projects, I explain the necessity for Ethics Committee approval
and talk about problems involved in undergraduates' procuring subjects or
being given too much freedom in interacting with children or parents. I
inform students about the availability of useful movies and videotapes.

GROUP MEETING TO DISCUSS REGISTRATION
AND REGULATIONS

Once preregistration lists are ready, I meet with the students and
explain, to the best of my knowledge, the UNC "system" for course reg-
istration and the vagaries of drop–add. I stress "going by the book"—that
is, doing whatever the main office deems appropriate. I discourage giving
undergraduates special permission to register until all official means have
been exhausted, and then I have the students get my approval before giving
such permission.

At this time, I also look over and discuss policies regarding grades and
examinations. All statements about grades are to be approved by me and
given to the students in writing. I have required that all students teaching
for the first time give two exams and a final in addition to a paper or project
assignment and that the first exam be within the first 5 weeks so that
student teachers get feedback about their performance as well as experience
in grading. I also recommend the use of quizzes or short assignments earlier
to facilitate this process. I require students to submit all exams and assignments for approval.

I refer the students to the Undergraduate Bulletin regarding the meaning of grades and discuss them at this time. I stress the problems of grade
inflation and point out that the grade of "C" should not be an uncommon
event. I state, of course, that all grades must be approved by me. It is my
experience that the more said about grades the better.

INDIVIDUAL AND GROUP MEETINGS

After the semester begins, I require students to see me once a week for the first month and periodically thereafter, to see how their lectures are going and to offer support and advice. In some years we have done this as a group, which is quite efficient as well as therapeutic. I think a group meeting of all the department's instructors once a week for the first month and every 2 weeks thereafter would be a major step forward.

EXAMINATION PROCEDURES

All questions are reviewed, and I discuss details such as number of questions (e.g., how many multiple-choice or essay), format, coverage from lecture and the textbook, and the point value for questions. Policies toward make-up exams are reviewed, and I offer them the option of "passing the buck" by telling their students that my approval is required before any change in policy can be made. This strategy works very well for minimizing hassles and excuses. Once exams are taken, students are to bring me examples of their grading—usually several "good" exams, "medium" ones, and "very poor" ones. Depending on the format, I have also graded exams as well. Once all exams are graded, we review the distribution and diagnose any problems. We also discuss any "problem" students and devise plans for handling them. The same procedures are used for the second exam and the final, although, depending on format, I may not ask to see as many actual exams.

SUGGESTIONS FOR THE FUTURE

Review of lecture materials. Although I usually spend considerable time explaining how I write lectures, and make mine available, I now think that all lecture notes should be reviewed. If nothing else, it would allow us to make sure that students are prepared and that they understand that lectures are not book reports.

Class visits. Students could make a videotape of themselves and then review it themselves or with me.

Lecture topics. In most instances, I have had no problems with the students' choices of topics. I have, on occasion, vetoed lectures that I was afraid might really be sermons, usually having to do with parenting, abortion, the Equal Rights Amendment, and so on. We might want to think about a carefully worded statement distinguishing the rights from the responsibilities of academic freedom.

Limits on research projects. I always worry about ethical implications of "thirdhand" supervision of research and have discouraged or disapproved many project proposals for this reason. We might want to consider the implications of undergraduates' working directly with children or parents under only a graduate student's authority. The same goes for student teachers bringing in subjects such as a parent and infant. I think such research activities need to be reviewed and supervised more directly.

Supervision of all students, experienced or otherwise. Because of the volunteer nature of my efforts, I have not had the time to follow the progress of older students' repeated efforts at teaching. Also, because of limited or nonexistent feedback about teaching success in past years, it has been hard to know how to certify teaching competency. I now think all teaching assistants need to be supervised and tracked, although to different degrees. Some of the problems with research projects and inflated grades have come from students who should have known better.

5

THE ETHICS OF THE SCIENTIFIC ENTERPRISE

Of the many kinds of research, I refer here to research that uses the scientific method, defined as the "principles and procedures for the systematic pursuit of knowledge involving the recognition and formulation of a problem, the collection of data through observation and experiment, and the formulation and testing of hypotheses" (*Webster's Ninth New Collegiate Dictionary*, 1983)—more simply referred to as empirical research.

Conducting research is often exciting and even thrilling, sometimes slow and laborious, on occasion frustrating and disappointing, but always governed by principles of ethical behavior. As highly regarded and valued as science is, just so closely is it duty-bound by a care for standards. In conducting research, psychologists owe a dual allegiance: on the one hand, to what is generally called the integrity of science; and, on the other, to the ethical principles governing research with humans and animals. In a word, psychologists face the special demands for ethical behavior incumbent on those who investigate behavior. It was just such a relationship that I was groping for when in 1982 I entitled a chapter "Ethics as an Integral Part of Research in Child Development" (Rheingold, 1982), a relationship now the province of the APA's newly formed Committee on Standards in Research (Grisso et al., 1991). Intimately related as these two sets of ethical principles are, for convenience I shall treat them separately.

HONOR IN SCIENCE

Until recently, the standards governing the pursuit of science were exemplified in the work of respected scientists, and were all the more binding because largely unwritten. We had tended to take the standards for granted, assuming that they would be learned without explicit tutelage and that our students would acquire them if only by our behavior in supervising their research. Yet the occurrence of some recent transgressions and the uncovering of past transgressions (Broad & Wade, 1982) have shown the need to enunciate the ideals. Sigma Xi, the Scientific Research Society, responded by publishing *Honor in Science* in 1984 and *A New Agenda for Science* in 1987. Among similar declarations by other professional and learned societies, I found especially informative the National Academy of Sciences bulletin (1989), *On Being a Scientist*. Parenthetically, I do not intend to imply that only in our research endeavors are we held to exacting ethical standards; they hold in equal measure for us as teachers, as scholars, and more generally as members of a profession.

With these paragraphs as preamble, I turn to the standards that will guide you in your research and scholarly endeavors because you are now entering into a solemn trust with standards to be enforced by no one but yourself.

The first principle requires that you acknowledge the source of your ideas, that is, the thoughts and work of others on whom your own efforts build. I do not mean just a pro forma listing of references in a paper but a thorough knowledge of the relevant literature—from the earliest to the most recent—coupled with a keen awareness of the ideas you gather from your colleagues and students. Granted, we do not always know where our ideas and research questions come from, nor can we always trace the precise path of our mental associations; still, the attempt must be made so that we do not claim undeserved priority for any of our efforts. All of us stand on the shoulders of others, even if they are not always giants, and we deserve scant credit for seeing and knowing more than our forebears—in time, even more than our mentors. Not to be scrupulously honest in acknowledging our intellectual debts constitutes plagiarism, misconduct sternly condemned and never condoned.

A second principle requires you to acknowledge in your talks and writing the contribution of others to your own efforts. Only in this way can your own contribution be weighed. A corollary of this principle demands that when others give you credit, you ensure that you are credited with no more than what you yourself think you contributed. Be especially mindful of the help and ideas you have received from your assistants and students. Also, the research community expects that coauthors, by accepting credit, bear responsibility for the entire report.

The third principle concerns the trustworthiness of your findings. The extent to which we are solely responsible for the trustworthiness of our data became clear to me early in my research career and actually shocked me into such awareness. Critical and demanding of the procedure and the conclusions as my dissertation examiners were, neither my advisor nor any member of the committee checked the raw scores of my findings, the techniques of data reduction, or the statistical analyses. They trusted my honesty! Again, the burden of personal responsibility startled me when I gave a technician a sheaf of hand-drawn figures to produce in the form required by the Graduate School, and he just reproduced my data points without referring to the scores I had supplied. No one but I was responsible for the accuracy of those points! It was a sobering experience.

In the first instance, trustworthiness is assured by your scrupulously carrying out the research operations exactly as stated. If you change a procedure in the midst of a study, be sure to report the change. It also means being constantly on guard so that less obvious, apparently minor changes do not occur during the course of the study. Trustworthiness applies as well to the accuracy of your data: elementary is the tenet that the computations must be checked and rechecked, for otherwise they are without value. Just so, there must be no evidence of *fraud*, *fabrication*, or *falsification*, today's terms for causes of concern—terms that remind me of Babbage's (1830/1971) concern for what he called "species of imposition" contributing to the decline of science. *Hoaxing* he defined as deceptions "without the accompaniment of wit"; *forging*, as the recording of observations never made; *trimming*, as the clipping off of little bits here and there from observations that are greater than the mean and sticking them onto those too small; and *cooking*, as giving observations the appearance of the highest degree of accuracy by, for example, selecting out of multitudes of observations only those that agree (pp. 174–183).

Babbage's *hoaxing* would fit today's *fraud*, except that lawyers at a workshop on scientific fraud and misconduct urged that *fraud* be used only in its legal sense, because the term specifies intent on the part of the perpetrator, and intent is difficult to prove (American Association for the Advancement of Science–American Bar Association National Conference of Lawyers and Scientists, 1989). His *forging* resembles today's *fabrication*, whereas *trimming* and *cooking* resemble today's *falsification*. With amusement, I note his judgment that trimming is perhaps not so injurious to truth as cooking, "except to the character of the trimmer" (p. 178).

Last but not least, the scientific enterprise rests on open communication and the free exchange of ideas. The phrase "publish or perish" is used only in a limited sense by the young professor awaiting tenure; more generally, it should mean that unless the work is made public, it perishes, and curtails the flow of ideas. We publish so others may confirm, correct, and extend our findings. Much work, it is true, deserves no more than filing in a bottom drawer, but precisely documented and trustworthy data are owed to the scientific community and the general public. Only in that open forum can the scientific enterprise be self-correcting and in turn, progressive.

I have opened this section with a relatively straightforward presentation of the ethical standards of science because now that you are no longer under the guidance of your professors, you are your own agent of control. True, science is self-correcting, but don't be the one to be corrected because of carelessness. Given that by the nature of the scientific enterprise there is no sure and certain way to proceed, you yourself must adhere to the standards to maintain the quality of your research. Finally, it is trust that supports the scientific enterprise. My professors trusted me, and their trust not only made me trustworthy but taught me to trust my students. So, too, do investigators trust each other; although we do not always agree with everyone's procedures or conclusions, we trust that they carried out the operations as they said they did and that they worked with care and diligence. Our knowledge, corrected and refined by generations of scientists, has accumulated by just that trust. Happily, society in general trusts the work of scientists. Science, then, rests on your integrity.

Indeed, I take satisfaction in Gerald Holton's (1986) judgment that "the occasional report of fraud or error is only the dark side of a coin, the reverse side of which is entirely bright" (p. 239). It behooves us, nevertheless, not only to honor all the ethical principles but also, and unhappily, to see that our colleagues do so as well. If you observe an act of scientific misconduct or of disregard for the rights and welfare of a research subject, you cannot ignore it. If you have reason to be concerned, you should consult your department chair or the dean informally and in confidence. From them you will learn your school's procedure for dealing with the allegation. True, no one wants to be a whistle-blower, but we are honor-bound to uphold the integrity of science.

HONORING YOUR SUBJECTS

The second set of ethical principles governs the conduct of research with human and animal subjects. The major tenet holds that the rights and welfare of participants must be respected; at the same time, a no less important tenet holds that the research should contribute to knowledge. Investigators, for their part, have the right to conduct research that increases knowledge and contributes to human and animal welfare, but that right is circumscribed by obligations to the participants. Although restraints on the rights of investigators can impede the search for knowledge, and unnecessary restraints could exact a grievous cost, nevertheless, investigators are constrained by these principles of ethical behavior in the conduct of their efforts. The principles have become ever more explicit and today are formally enunciated in governmental regulations and professional codes of ethics. As a result, the moment you conceive the barest outline of the study you wish to perform, in the next you must be sure that your procedures honor the principles.

RESEARCH WITH HUMAN PARTICIPANTS

As evidence of our increased ethical sensitivity, I begin by noting that the recent statement of the APA's ethical principles (1992) uses the term *participants* rather than the formerly more common term *subjects*. Although day by day we become increasingly concerned about the rights of people as research subjects, the concerns have a long history. Indeed, the APA began setting standards for the behavior of psychologists from the beginning, and the Belmont Report (National Commission for Protection of Human Subjects of Biomedical and Behavioral Research, 1979) refers to the Nüremberg Code of 1947, to the Helsinki Declaration of 1964, and, centuries earlier, to the Hippocratic maxim of 400 B.C., "do no harm."

What are the rights of participants? They include the right to be informed about the purpose of the study, the right to privacy, the right to be treated with respect and dignity, the right to be protected from physical and mental harm, the right to choose to participate or to refuse without prejudice or reprisals, the right to anonymity in the reporting of results, and the right to the safeguarding of their records. Nor do people abdicate their rights by consenting to participate, because they may withdraw from the study at any time. Some of these rights, however, require special consideration. In particular, infants and very young children cannot give consent, nor can the mentally infirm, because they would not have full knowledge of what their participation entails; for their study, permission must be obtained from their parents or guardians (Society for Research in Child Development, 1990). And for all persons, consent is not enough; it must be informed consent.

Obtaining Informed Consent

In the first step of obtaining informed consent, whether by letter, telephone call, or in person, identify yourself, your professional status, and your institution. Inasmuch as such identification confers a measure of respect and even power, be sensitive to how much easier it generally is for people to acquiesce with requests than to refuse them. No one likes to risk the disapproval of an apparently important person. So, identification notwithstanding, a bit of humility is in order.

Next, state the purpose of the study, that is, what you seek to learn and why it is important. Use everyday words that people will understand,

and not the technical jargon of the laboratory. People are also entitled to know why they have been selected (e.g., by age, sex, or educational status) and how you obtained their names. Now tell them what they will be asked to do (for example, to play with their children, memorize lists, judge stories, or fill out a questionnaire); how long the task will take; and then, depending on your plan, whether you wish to see them more than once.

So far, I have given a bare minimum of the opening steps that precede your asking the persons if they are willing to cooperate with your request. Let your tone of voice or the phrasing of the letter convey the sense of a request and not a command, and a request so phrased that refusal would be easy. At the end of your letter or conversation, assure the persons that the information they contribute will be held in confidence and that, because all records are filed by code numbers, they as individuals will remain anonymous. You are now taking the first steps in honoring what is meant by *informed consent*.

One question continues to trouble me: in obtaining informed consent, how fully should you state the purpose of your study? I recommend a general statement in everyday language, because too academic a statement might not be understood, and too detailed a one might alter, distort, or inhibit the participants' normal behavior. For example, people might rehearse their responses beforehand, or parents tutor their children. Less-than-full disclosure, then, becomes a matter of judgment depending on what you are studying; as such, the practice is condoned by the need to obtain unbiased, representative behavior. Here, as elsewhere, when in doubt, consult not only your colleagues but also a person or parent of the population you plan to study. Consider, also, using the opportunity at the beginning of the actual study, as you chat with the participants, to repeat, or give more information about, the purpose and procedures of the study.

In contrast, I consider it unethical to misinform a participant about the purpose of the study. To deceive participants I judge unacceptable, not because it may make people suspicious of scientists, nor because it may embarrass them, nor yet because it erodes our own self-concept, but because it betrays the trust of each person in the other. At the least, informed consent is belied. Let us remember that in everyday life, lying is wrong; so, too, should it be in the scientific enterprise.

Not all behavioral scientists agree, however. For those who believe that the use of deception is justified, the APA code offers cautionary guidelines as well as advice for treating a participant's discomfort at being deceived. So controversial and difficult is the issue that I advise you to seek guidance before proceeding with such a study and to seek it conscientiously from persons holding opposing values. Nevertheless, let us now consider adding the giving of false information about the purpose of a study to the many kinds of procedures we should not use. Just as respect for life has forced us to be creative in devising ways to study human behavior, so, too, we should be able to discover ways to gain information without deception.

Documenting Informed Consent

Now, all the information you have given the participants to obtain cooperation must be presented to them in writing, together with your name and telephone number and the name and number of your institution's designated official. Participants sign one copy for your records and keep one for themselves. Even if no risk of any kind is involved and oral consent has been judged sufficient, still the participant should be given a written description of the research, its purpose and procedures, your name and phone number, and the name and number of your campus's official.

When children are the participants, the consent forms are signed by their parents or guardians. Even then, children are not to be coerced: As soon as they are able to understand, they should be told what they are asked to do and that they are free to participate or not; later, as they are able to read and write, they, too, may sign a more simply worded *assent* form. Bear in mind, however, that although children as young as 5 years of age understand what you are asking them to do, even older children appear not to understand what giving assent means (Abramovitch, Freedman, Thoden, & Nikolich, 1991). For example, knowing that their parents have consented to their participation, how can the children refuse? Or, despite the experimenter's customary assurance of confidentiality, how can children really believe that their parents could not find out how they performed?

When the children to be studied are in a center or a school, a third agency of consent, in addition to the parents and the children, is required. Many preschools and most schools have their own guidelines for you to follow in requesting permission and approval for your study. In the Supplement at the end of this chapter, Lynne Baker-Ward describes the many steps to conducting research in such settings.

The Investigator—Subject Partnership

The attitude you assume toward your participants can do much to honor their rights. You will of course treat them, children no less than adults, with courtesy, respect, and esteem for freely volunteering their time and person for what amounts to an invasion of their privacy. But you can go one step further and recognize them—even children—as partners in the search for knowledge. Without affecting the behavior under study, you can talk informally of your own research interests and endeavors and give them examples of how science proceeds to answer questions. When subjects see their role in the larger enterprise, their self-esteem is enhanced and their cooperation assured.

As you begin to gather data, be sure to tell the participants of any hidden devices by which you may be recording their behavior. Because they should not be under surveillance without their knowledge, now is the time to point out any one-way windows, microphones, or closed-circuit TV cameras and to explain who may be not only the hidden observers but also the eventual coders of the records. At this time, too, you can explain (as well as include in the consent form) that if any tapes or records are to be used for demonstration—in a class or seminar—you will first ask for their permission.

During the study, guard against remarking on some personal characteristic of the child or adult that may seem innocent enough to you, and even complimentary, but may be otherwise interpreted by the recipient and especially by the parent. On the other hand, every participant should leave the study with a sense of accomplishment, and here I am talking not about foolish praise but rather genuine appreciation. In truth, no participant can fail, because what is at test is your hypothesis, not the participant's performance. Thus, if participants ask how well they did, take the asking as a warning that you did not sufficiently inform them about the questing nature of research at the beginning of the study or sufficiently reassure them during it. Be mindful, too, of your role as an investigator so that you do not slip unwittingly into that of counselor or therapist.

Once you begin to regard your participants as partners, you realize how entitled they are to learn the results of their participation. Although too often this responsibility goes unacknowledged, you should consider sending them a clear and simple statement of the study's main findings. In this connection I prepared the parents of my studies for the form a scientist's findings take—for example, the use of means and measures of variation that obscure any one individual's contribution.

Obtaining Formal Approval

All persons who plan to study human behavior must submit their proposals, even for pilot studies, to a formally constituted ethical review board, and often to more than one. Therefore, as you prepare your proposal, study the established ethical principles to be sure that your procedures violate none of the standards set by your institution, your professional societies, and the Code of Federal Regulations (45 CFR 46). From these, you learn the absolutely binding principle that, formal approval notwithstanding, the final responsibility for ethical practices is yours. Furthermore, you are responsible also for those of your assistants and students, all of whom incur similar obligations. The latter point reminds you to instruct them in ethical practices, as well as to monitor their performance throughout the course of a study.

Although the steps you take to gain formal approval will differ by institution, I outline those you would follow to conduct research in an academic setting. First, you submit your proposal to the professors of the department's ethical review committee. My department's form for requesting a review asks for a description of the proposed study and the participants, and then for the following information:

1. Are the subjects at risk, that is, exposed to the possibility of physical, mental, or social discomfit, harm, or danger? If so, describe steps taken to minimize the possibility, and if necessary, attach a justification for these procedures based on the scientific literature.
2. How will prior informed consent be obtained?
3. Is deception involved?
4. Are there anticipated benefits to subjects or society?
5. What are the security procedures for assuring the participants' privacy and the confidentiality of the data?

At the end, you sign that you have read and will abide by the APA's (1992) Standards for Research With Human Participants (from the *Ethical Principles*), and agree to report any significant changes to the committee for additional review.

If the ethics committee approves the proposal, the department's head forwards it to your school's institutional review board (IRB) for final approval before any data can be collected. The board's province covers all research proposed by any student or faculty member, whether or not supported by outside funds. Among the main concerns of the IRB are assurances that a participant's identity is protected and that participants are informed about every detail of the study that might influence their willingness to cooperate. The members of such a board respect their charge: to observe the participants' rights while they preserve the researchers' freedom of inquiry. Interestingly, Charles R. McCarthy, director of the federal Office for Protection from Research Risks, at a workshop in 1991 expressed the opinion that institutional review boards are a major American cultural contribution, unique in the world.

In some instances, you must seek approval from still other boards of ethical review. For example, if you apply for a grant, granting agencies review proposals not only for scientific merit but also for adherence to ethical standards. In fact, one condition of funding is prior approval by the aforementioned institutional review boards. Were you to conduct research with human participants in an environment not providing ethical review boards, you would nevertheless be governed by the ethical principles of the federal regulations and your professional society. Consider asking the review board of a nearby university, institute, or hospital to review your proposal, or instead, you might consider convening your own board of reviewers. Here you should be guided by the federal regulations that the board be composed of at least five members of different backgrounds and expertise, including one person not affiliated with your institution and another whose primary concerns are in a nonscientific area. In the end, however, the responsibility to observe the rights of others is always yours.

Using Undergraduates as Subjects

Over the years, students in undergraduate courses in psychology have provided a convenient sample for study by professors and graduate students. In fact, much—and according to some critics, too much—of what we have learned about human behavior is based on that of freshmen and sophomores. The gain to knowledge aside, participating in a study gives students firsthand experience with the empirical procedures of the behavioral sciences, and such experience brings a measure of life to the facts and principles they learn from lectures and textbooks. Besides, no sample of subjects better qualifies as partners in the search for knowledge.

If you plan to gain such data, just remember that undergraduates are also human beings and thus are entitled to all the rights spelled out for the conduct of research with human participants. Their participation cannot be made a requirement for completing the course, violating as it would the principle of voluntary consent. To honor that principle, you must inform students of the research requirement before they enroll in the course; this notice is often given in the catalog (at UNC at Chapel Hill, it appears thus: "Students participate in ongoing research in the Department"). Then, during the first class meeting, tell them how many hours of participation are required, the probable nature of the projects from which they may choose, the alternatives to participating as a subject (e.g., to summarize selected research reports or to assist in a professor's research project), and their right to drop out of a given research project at any time without penalty. As befits their status as students and above all as partners in the enterprise, tell them the purpose of the study, its procedures, and the results as soon as they are compiled. No less is demanded to provide an instructive experience. Not only are the students contributing to knowledge, but they are learning how such contributions are gained. So, too, do they learn of the ethical principles governing research with human participants. It goes without saying that the proposals for all such projects would have been reviewed and approved by the department's ethical committee and the appropriate institutional review board.

RESEARCH WITH ANIMALS

A moment's thought reveals how different is the status of nonhuman animals as subjects of research. Their consent to be studied, let alone informed consent, cannot be gained. They are not free to choose to participate, nor to withdraw during a study. No constitution guarantees them a bill of rights. Instead, their use depends on us who as moral persons are responsible for treating them humanely. As a result, the rules and regulations for their use appear to be even more numerous and more stringent than those governing the study of human beings.

Recent, often vociferous, criticism of the use of animals in scientific research notwithstanding, concern for the welfare of these animals has a long history (Dewsbury, 1990). Within this century, controversy touched the research of such luminaries as Robert M. Yerkes, G. Stanley Hall, John B. Watson, Ivan P. Pavlov, and Edward L. Thorndike. Indeed, as early as 1925—I take pride in noting—the APA adopted a series of resolutions proposed by its Committee on Precautions in Animal Experimentation, of which Paul Thomas Young (1928) was chairman. Of the many recommendations, I found these especially noteworthy: (a) Animals in the laboratory shall receive every consideration for their bodily comfort; (b) they shall be kindly treated, properly fed, and their surroundings kept in the best possible sanitary condition; (c) the same care shall be taken to minimize an animal's discomfort after an operation, as in a hospital for human beings; (d) psychology journals should require that manuscripts describing experiments with animals contain explicit statements about measures taken to avoid needless pain or discomfort, and decline to publish manuscripts of studies that violate the association's code; and (e) the association should maintain a standing committee. A concluding paragraph stated, "Since psychologists today are using animals for experimental purposes it follows that they should assume part of the responsibility of protecting scientific investigation against unenlightened statements and legal enactment" (p. 489).

Today, the treatment of animals in research is regulated not only by the APA's current *Guidelines for Ethical Conduct in the Care and Use of Animals* (1985) and those of other scientific societies (e.g., Animal Behavior Society, 1986; Sigma Xi, Committee on Science and Society, 1991) but also by federal, state, and local laws—the legal enactment foreshadowed by the 1925 Committee on Precautions. Indeed, as psychologists studying the behavior of animals, we did not wait on civil laws to behave ethically!

What are these rules and regulations? In the first instance, you are responsible for the care and housing of your animals to ensure their physical and psychological well-being and also for enriching their environment as appropriate. The most recent (1990) amendment to the Animal Welfare

Act of 1966 goes further in recommending group living for dogs and primates.

Then, before you can begin to gather data, just as with the study of human subjects, you must obtain the approval of your campus review board—for animals, labeled the Institutional Animal Care and Use Committee. This committee not only inspects your laboratory twice a year but also assures that your study complies with all the regulations and guidelines. In seeking the committee's approval you are asked to state the main objectives of your study and to tell why the species you plan to study is the most appropriate as well as the least likely to suffer from what you plan to do. You are further asked if there will be a need to distress your subjects, to use drugs, or to perform surgery, and what you will do to relieve their distress. (Indeed, you must use sedation, analgesia, or anesthesia if you cause the animals more than slight pain or distress. Psychologists are in fact encouraged to test painful stimuli on themselves.)

The guidelines of both the APA and the Animal Behavior Society alert you to more imaginative and less stressful ways of studying some behaviors of interest, such as using positive rather than aversive stimuli to evoke behavior, or studying aggression and predation in natural encounters of free-living animals in the field rather than in staged conflicts. But field studies themselves, of course, are not entirely free of ethical problems, because they can disrupt the normal behavior of the animals and their associates (Cuthill, 1991).

The committee also wants to know how many animals you will need for your study—a question meant to encourage you to use fewer animals, but one which should be carefully and precisely answered in terms of what you are trying to show and the experimental design guiding your efforts. Too few animals could result in an experiment of low power that would, in fact, waste those you did use. As courses in statistics and design teach us, with knowledge of certain parameters we can determine the minimum number of subjects needed to produce answers of acceptable power. Therefore, show the committee that the number of animals you plan to use rests on sound scientific practice.

Finally, we are urged by our own ethical guidelines and those of other agencies (e.g., American Association for the Advancement of Science, 1990; Sigma Xi, 1991; U.S. Congress, Office of Technology Assessment, 1986) to consider the possibility of using alternatives to animals. Can your questions be answered by computer modeling or by tissue and cell cultures? At the present time, however, and perhaps for a long time, many questions we ask will require an intact living organism.

BEYOND THE GUIDELINES

We can become so impressed with our attempts to advance knowledge that we think—as I did some years ago—that the finest act any person could engage in would be to serve as a subject in whatever psychologists propose to study. But now I see that act as a gift—of a person's time, behavior, thoughts, and wishes—given out of kindness and faith in our endeavors. Therefore, we must always entertain the possibility that enthusiasm for the product of our minds, and convictions about the value of our research, could blind us to the rights and welfare of those we study. Even the best designed study does not justify our violating the rights and welfare of others. As you become increasingly sensitive to the matter, questions about your own practices will come to mind. To resolve them, freely consult others, going beyond colleagues in your own discipline to those in others, as well as to laypersons. Would you serve as a subject in that study? Would you have your child so serve? Are you willing to test on yourself the painful stimuli you apply to an animal? Realize, furthermore, that even as your current efforts do now conform to the established ethical principles, codes are living documents, open to new amendments and regulations for guiding your future efforts. Be alert to changes. Be your own severest critic as you become ever more sensitive to the needs of others, both human and non-human.

PASSING THE LAST CHECKPOINT

Today the editors of our journals (e.g., *American Psychologist, Animal Behaviour, Child Development, Psychological Science, Science*) also assume responsibility for upholding the principles that guide our scholarly and research efforts. To protect the integrity of science, editors require that all persons you list as authors of your manuscript have agreed to be so listed, that they have seen and approved the manuscript, and that they are responsible for its contents. They caution you not to submit a previously published manuscript nor one under review by another journal. Furthermore, you are required to keep the raw data for at least 5 years after your manuscript is published. A more instructive statement appears in the APA *Publication Manual* (1983):

> It is traditional in scientific publication to retain data, instructions, details of procedure, and analyses so that copies may be made available in response to inquiries from interested readers. Therefore, you are encouraged to retain these materials for a minimum of 5 years after your article has been published. (p. 163)

I find this statement all the more powerful because it is so matter-of-fact.

Editors also require evidence that you honored the ethical principles of research with human and animal subjects. As I pointed out earlier, in 1925 the APA Committee on Precautions in Animal Experimentation was already asking journal editors to decline manuscripts of experiments that violated its code (Young, 1928). Today the practice is well-nigh uniform. You must accompany your manuscript with a statement that you have observed all relevant ethical principles—informed consent, and all that it implies, from human participants, and humane care and use of animals.

The "last checkpoint" is not the best figure of speech for this section because in fact it is the first checkpoint. Keep it in mind as you plan your study.

SUPPLEMENT

GUIDELINES FOR CONDUCTING RESEARCH IN CHILD CARE CENTERS

LYNNE BAKER-WARD

North Carolina State University

September 1991

The following guidelines, developed over the past decade of studying the cognitive development of more than 500 young children in numerous preschools, day-care centers, public and private elementary schools, and after-school programs, have proved helpful in securing the cooperation of parents, children, and child care directors and staff.

LOCATING A STUDY SITE

Once a new research proposal has been approved by the appropriate university authorities, we set about finding a site whose director is willing to participate. We consult the local organizations concerned with child care for information on the day-care centers in the community. We try to avoid any that have just opened, those undergoing accreditation or any other investigation, and those whose directors are new to their jobs.

When we have selected a possible site, rather than describing the project over the telephone, we make an appointment with its director to discuss our research. A scheduled appointment permits a fuller exposition of the research and allows the director to consider the request without interruptions.

OBTAINING THE DIRECTOR'S CONSENT

To prepare for the first meeting with a director, the students and I write a brief summary of the project, stating the research questions, why they are important, the procedures we will carry out, and how the data will answer the questions. We include a list of what we will ask that the site provide: (a) the numbers and ages of the children we want to study; (b) the type of space we need; (c) the amount of time required; and (d) the staff members (if any) to help us. Also, we draft a "parent letter" and consent form (see p. 67). We find it helpful to take samples of the research materials (e.g., the pictures to be used as the to-be-remembered items, or the objects children will be given to reenact an event such as a visit to the doctor) so that the director can see the exact tasks we will present to the children.

At the meeting, we go over the materials we have brought and answer questions. If the director continues to be interested in participating, we explore the compatibility of the site's facilities and timetable with our own needs: Will there be mutually convenient times for data collection? Will an appropriate space be available? How will the children be escorted to and from their classrooms?

If the situation appears to be workable, we ask how to obtain formal permission. In some centers, the director can grant permission; in others, a board of directors evaluates the director's recommendation; and in still others, the entire staff decides. In the latter case, we offer to attend staff meetings to present the research and to answer questions.

SELECTING THE CHILDREN

In our discussion with the director, we define the criteria for subject selection: the preferred age or gender distribution or the desirability of excluding children with certain learning or behavioral problems. To avoid violating confidentiality by asking for specific information about a particular child, we ask the director simply to tell us which children fit our requirements.

OBTAINING THE PARENTS' CONSENT

Once formal permission has been granted by the director of the site, we need permission from the parents. For this, we ask the director to review our "parent letter" and to suggest any changes. The content of this letter is so important that we also consult nonpsychologist parents and incorporate their suggestions along with the director's.

The parent letter contains much of the information presented in the research proposal. Here, however, the emphasis is on answering questions that parents are more likely to ask—so that while we try to give a clear and accurate statement of the research, we omit discussion of the more arcane and academic issues. We nevertheless invite parents to ask for additional information. (When it seems useful, we provide the center with copies of published articles on our research, which the parents may consult.)

The following questions are most frequently asked by parents and should therefore be addressed in the parent letter:

- How can I be sure that the research is legitimate and that the researchers are competent?
- How was my child selected for the study? Are all the children in my child's class being recruited, or is some particular feature of my child's background or characteristics relevant?
- What exactly will my child be asked to do? Will additional requests be made of my child or of me?
- Will participation in this study disrupt my child's day at school?
- What happens if I say my child does not wish to take part after I have consented?
- How will information about my child be used?
- How will confidentiality be assured?
- What can I learn about my child's performance in this task?

Because many parents have unrealistic expectations about psychological research, we take special care to be clear about the feedback we can provide. A statement in the letter informs them that only group results are reported and that, although we are happy to discuss a particular child's responses, we cannot interpret them because we are learning about the range of typical behavior rather than evaluating individuals. If the research includes a lengthy interview or the discussion of a potentially sensitive topic, we offer the parents an opportunity to observe our interactions with their children. In some cases, we offer to provide them with videotapes of their children's interviews; when funds for extra tapes are not available, we offer to copy the interviews on tapes they provide.

We have found it useful to ask parents to indicate on the consent form whether they do or do not want their children to take part in the study, and to return it in either case. We then feel free to send additional reminders to those who do not return the forms, and thus we can be sure that all parents have actually received the letter.

The director's approval of the project is usually stated in the first paragraph. In some cases directors choose to send the letter over their signature or to add a statement and their signature to the bottom of the letter. The parent letter is then distributed in the manner suggested by the director. In most cases, it goes home with the children; in others, it is mailed to their homes or distributed at parent meetings.

OBTAINING THE CHILDREN'S ASSENT

Before the actual study begins, we meet the children individually and make sure that each one is willing to participate. To that end we meet with the teachers to discuss the study and the scheduling and to examine the space that we will be using. We then ask the teachers to select the first participants from among the more outgoing children, to introduce us to them by name, and to tell them that we will be asking them some questions to learn more about boys and girls their age. The children are told that they can choose to interact with the examiners or not, and that they have their parents' permission to talk to them if they wish to do so.

In our experience, very few children refuse to respond to the examiner when the above approach has been used. If a child does not wish to participate, we respect that wish and say that we will ask again later. If there is hesitation at the second invitation, we change the setting as much as possible to make the child more comfortable. For example, we may ask a teacher's assistant to accompany the child, or we may conduct the study closer to the child's classroom. If the child still does not wish to participate, we simply thank him or her and go on to the next one.

WORKING WITH THE CENTER

One of our goals is, as far as possible, to make some contribution to the research site while we are conducting the study. For example, in some cases when the data were to be collected with videorecording equipment and the center did not own such equipment, we visited the center beforehand to tape children performing some activity of interest to the director. This practice helped us, too, because the children became familiar with us before we started to make requests of them.

In other cases, we have conducted workshops with the staff on the topic of our research. As all child care workers in North Carolina must obtain a certain number of hours of in-service training each year, such sessions represent a tangible contribution to the center. At the same time, the feedback received from the staff at the end of the study has proved useful (e.g., discussion with teachers on the nature of the curriculum has led to hypotheses about the development of memory strategies, and teachers' suggestions have enabled us to word instructions more appropriately). Furthermore, graduate students, by participating in such workshops, also receive valuable training in how to explain research findings to nonacademic persons.

Participating in research activities is often quite enjoyable and special to children, and those who do not serve as subjects may feel left out. To avoid having any child feel uncomfortable, we work out a plan with the director to provide all children with some special experience (subject, of course, to their parents' wishes). For example, children who are not subjects can accompany the researcher or a staff member to the testing room for a simulated interview (where no data are collected) so that they, too, can have a turn; if this plan involves contact with the researchers, rather than the staff, it should be discussed in the parent letter because parental consent is necessary. In other cases, a classroom activity has been provided so that all children can interact with an interesting piece of research equipment; for example, when data are collected on a microcomputer, the apparatus can be set up in the classroom and all children can enjoy experimenting with age-appropriate software. Similarly, if stickers or other tokens are to be given to the subjects, we develop a plan with the teachers to give them to the nonparticipating children as well.

Shortly after data collection begins, we make a point of asking the director if the staff have expressed any concerns or made any suggestions about the research procedures. The director is encouraged to call the supervising faculty member with questions or comments at any time throughout the study. Any questions from parents are answered promptly.

As the study proceeds, contacting the director every few weeks throughout the study helps to solve minor difficulties and to coordinate upcoming schedules.

COMPLETING THE WORK

We send a thank-you letter to the staff shortly after the data have been collected and then send a brief summary of the results to the center as soon as possible (we also send this to the parents who requested one, even though the minor analyses may not have been completed). When a report of the study is prepared for publication, we ask the director for permission to acknowledge the center by name. Copies of all conference papers and publications are sent to the center.

If we wish to show, at a professional meeting, videotapes of subjects performing a task, we ask for the parents' consent even though the children are not identified on the tape. The parents are told why the tape was selected (e.g., "Your child's performance was representative of her age group, and the quality of the recording was particularly excellent"); they are sent a copy of the videotape in question; and they are asked to sign and return a letter of consent.

PROCEDURES FOR CONDUCTING RESEARCH IN PUBLIC SCHOOLS

With minor modifications, the procedures outlined above for working with day-care centers apply to working in public or private school settings as well. The initial contact is usually with the administrative office of the school system, where frequently there is a research officer to handle such requests. The administrator may be able to grant approval as a designee of the school system, or action by a committee may be required. The school administrators will need to see the questionnaires or other instruments to be used, along with all consent letters. In any case, we budget ample time for the request to be reviewed.

With permission from the school system we can begin to contact principals, following suggestions from the research officer and from principals we have worked with in the past. Procedures for obtaining the principal's consent and conducting the research parallel those discussed earlier.

An additional concern in working with school-age children is using information from the students' school records. For example, many researchers wish to use achievement or intelligence test scores to describe the sample or to compare different groups of subjects. Particular caution should be exercised in obtaining such confidential information. In many cases when standardized test scores are desired, it may be preferable for investigators to administer their own assessments. If, however, information collected by the schools is needed, parental consent must be obtained. Furthermore, the assistance of the administration is necessary, as only school personnel should extract the information from the students' files. To safeguard confidentiality, the information should be obtained only after the research has been completed so that it can be identified by subject numbers rather than names. When parents are asked to release information from their children's records, they should be given clear explanations of the reasons for the request and informed of the confidentiality safeguards.

The consent of school-age children is as important as the assent of younger ones. We explain the nature of the research to them and give them ample opportunities to raise questions. At the end of the study, we tell the children about the results we obtained. We think this feedback session is a useful educational experience for even primary school children; it also serves an important function in allaying any concerns they may have about their performance or about the "true" purpose of the research.

SUMMARY

The general principles guiding our efforts include the following:

- Careful planning of all procedures and contacts

- Full cooperation with administration and staff
- Gentle handling of children and their parents
- Maintaining confidentiality
- Providing information to all involved—before, during, and after the study
- Enriching the study sites by research-related contributions to their needs

6

THE PURSUIT OF RESEARCH

In this chapter I turn to some practical matters of the research enterprise, always under the aegis of ethical standards. Of a host of possible issues, I discuss a few: Some treat ideas, others are cautions and hints, and a few are by-the-way thoughts. In the first place, any advice is limited by how unchartable are the seas of discovery. In Szent-Györgi's (1971) words, "research means going out into the unknown with the hope of finding something new to bring home" (p. 1). True, hope sustains, but to bolster that hope, all of us can use some help in planning the voyage. Although, as a voyage into the unknown, its course cannot be compassed by any fixed set of rules, nevertheless there are many to guide its course.

THE TOPIC OF YOUR RESEARCH

Let me start at the moment when the topic of your new research flashes into your mind. In blinding clarity you see what you wish to study and the enormous contribution it will make to knowledge. Enjoy your exhilaration as long as you can, because it must sustain you through the arduous effort of bringing that insight to earth. As the first moment passes, a host of questions come tumbling into mind. What exactly shall you measure, and in whom? What shall you vary and what hold constant? And how shall all the factors be related?

From the beginning, try to cast your idea in the broadest possible framework. What abstract principle will your efforts illustrate? What theory of behavior will they support or negate? What change in our thinking will they force? Just to gather data is no feat; to try to figure out what they may possibly mean is a feat, but not a trustworthy one. Think boldly. Stretch your imagination. What will your results mean, what will be their significance? So, early on, try to place your idea in the larger scheme of knowledge, for this, too, will sustain you through the vicissitudes ahead, especially as you come to realize that you can work on only some small part of that glittering whole.

How do you arrive at the topic that sustains the dream? By now, you know the area within which you will work and many characteristics of the subjects, human or animal. For a few years, you could easily pursue some leads uncovered in your dissertation; after all, you know the literature and have perfected a method. Nevertheless, after a study or two, try to move beyond your dissertation. Medawar (1979) cautioned against continuing your doctoral work for the rest of your life, "easy and tempting though it is to tie up loose ends and wander down attractive byways" (p. 14). You could also pursue some questions related to your major professor's program of research. But, to be tied too long to an advisor's work shows a lack of originality and independence. Or, you could study a topic that is favored at the moment, one that granting agencies are advertising a readiness to support. Although, in general, you should resist fads, if you do have a burning interest in investigating a topic of current concern or a newly popular technique, do so, of course. By themselves, however, fashion and dollars do not always translate into a burning interest.

Furthermore, what are young investigators to do when the editor of a journal in which they might someday like to see their research published expresses a preference for manuscripts reporting on multiple studies, multiple methods, or behavior in multiple settings, or when granting agencies express a preference for multidisciplinary proposals? Might not young (and perhaps even seasoned) investigators accept the editor's and the granting agency's preference as a dictum to which they should tailor their research? Now, there is nothing wrong with conducting that recommended series of studies, or any of the other summa bona, but unless the research is contracted for, the pronouncements contravene the hallowed freedom of the scientific enterprise.

Journal editors and granting agencies are indeed free to express their view of the direction that the research they report or support ought to take. But despite the complexity of behavior, is it not conceivable that a study of only one or two variables, measured at only one time, could make a fundamental contribution to knowledge? Our science is not yet advanced to the stage where studies of many, often related variables, measured at different times and places in the lives of the subjects, are always interpretable, yielding, as they so often do, an intricate set of statistical relationships of low predictive power.

On balance, then, study whatever interests you deeply. If it does, it is bound to be important.

Basic and Applied Research

Of the many choices we make in planning and conducting research, two have interested me especially: the difference between basic and applied research as it determines the topic of one's research, and that between laboratory and field research as it determines the method of exploring that topic. Sharp and clear as these differences seem, in practice they often disappear.

In conducting basic research, we try to answer questions seemingly without regard for their immediate relation to problems vexing society. The questions originate with individuals themselves as they conduct experiments that Francis Bacon called studies of light, not fruit. But whether the outside world sees the significance of such studies for humankind or not, let us acknowledge that no matter how esoteric or obscure the topic may seem to an observer, to the investigator there is no questioning that significance.

In conducting applied research, we look for ways to treat or prevent a particular problem. The research is called for and supported by society. In contrast, basic research often comes under attack for its apparent lack of relevance to our pressing problems. Yet always the solution of these problems comes from fundamental knowledge gained by basic research. Again, applied research often demands large sums of money, as well as the efforts of many scientists, sometimes from several disciplines. In contrast, much basic science is small science, sensitively described by F. H. T. Rhodes, president of Cornell University, in his 1985 Annual Report, as "a precious and vulnerable thing. It is the private bewilderment, the personal hunch, the audacious extrapolation, the sudden intuition, the individual flare, that have been, and still are, the motivating forces for all fundamental science."

On close examination, however, the distinction between basic and applied research cannot be drawn, for what starts out to be the one becomes the other. The basic research of Roentgen, the Curies, and Fleming, to take the most illustrious examples, contributed beyond measure to the cure of ills. On the other side, Binet in 1904 was asked to organize special classes for retarded children—surely an applied problem—and to do so, he devised a scale of mental development. R. A. Fisher, in conducting agricultural experiments during the 1920s, developed statistical designs and tests used today by scientists in every discipline. More recently, Neal Miller (1983) showed how the field of behavioral medicine resulted from the fruitful interaction of basic science in the laboratory and applied science in the clinic.

What advice do I offer? Shall you conduct basic or applied research? On the one hand, do not choose applied research only because you can get the dollars; on the other, do not be put off from basic research because it solves no present pressing need of society. Just remember that if we go on applying what we now know, although we shall not run out of problems to solve, we shall one day run out of knowledge to solve them. My advice is: Investigate whatever is of burning interest to you.

The Laboratory and the Field

Just as distinctions between basic and applied research become blurred on examination, so do those between the laboratory and the field as the proper environment for the study of behavior. Today, at least in some quarters, laboratory studies appear to carry a freight of disfavor, as may be inferred from this description of the articles that the editorial board of the journal *Developmental Psychology* (1992, 28, 2) proposes to publish:

> In the case of laboratory experimental studies, preference is given to reports of series of studies, and the external validity of such studies is a major consideration. Field research, cross-cultural studies, research on gender and ethnicity, and research on other socially important topics are especially welcome.

This description suggests a judgment of the greater importance of one type over the other, as well as different standards for judging research procedures, the one more strict, the other, more lenient. The implied summum bonum here is ecological validity.

To be sure, posed so bluntly, the laboratory and the field are very different places and have very different properties. Yet each can be altered to acquire some properties of the other: For example, a laboratory may be not one room but a suite of rooms, it may be not cold or bare but warm and rich in furnishings and thus may mirror a student's dorm room or a family den.

Alternatively, perhaps, the difference between lab and field may lie not so much in the setting as in the amount or nature of experimental control. But I can visualize a day-care center as the locus of a tightly controlled study (I carried out such a study in an institution) and at the same time visualize a laboratory as the locus for free play. Control, then, need not be a distinguishing feature.

Recent concerns about ecological validity have characterized laboratory studies as artificial and without generalized significance. I often hear it said that in the lab, we study the strange behavior of children in strange situations with strange adults, a claim sure to surprise and even dismay the real (unfamiliar, to be sure, but not odd or peculiar) persons—students and professors alike—who have evoked friendly and imaginative and real behavior in a playroom in the laboratory, witness countless studies in the literature.

We need to be wise enough not to pit the one environment (or setting) against the other, but instead to see how each has value and, what is more, how they complement each other. An observation of behavior in the field of real life sparks the idea for a controlled study in the laboratory. Similarly, conclusions reached in the laboratory can be verified by observations in the field. When a creeping child in an airport deposited a toy in my lap, I and my students tested the generality of the phenomenon among toddlers by using many different kinds of objects, and recipients both familiar and unfamiliar, male and female, in the laboratory. Then we fanned out over the campus and the town and, in an afternoon, recorded 23 similar observations. The measure of a study is not the environment in which it is conducted—the laboratory or the field—but its contribution to knowledge. To conform to the temper of the times, let us not deride the laboratory, deny its special properties, or eschew its use. Similarly, let us not shun the theater of everyday life for fear of just following the fashion. Stay with your question. It will tell you the environment—or environments—in which to seek an answer.

HYPOTHESES AND DESIGNS

A truism states that research takes the form of questions put to nature. The questions are your hypotheses: What is the effect of a on b? How is b related to c? In seeking answers, you propose explanations. At this very point, you should stand far back from your own hypotheses and heed Thomas C. Chamberlin's (1890/1965) picturesque warning: "The moment one has offered an original explanation for a phenomenon which seems satisfactory, that moment affection for his intellectual child springs into existence; and as the explanation grows into a definite theory, his parental affections cluster around his intellectual offspring" (p. 755). Chamberlin cautioned that the investigator might then unwittingly select, and even magnify the importance of, evidence that supports the hypothesis and ignore what does not.

How can you prize your own great idea and at the same time question it? Yet, question it you must. You need not abandon it, but instead cast it as a possible, or more likely probable, hypothesis—as only one among several. Following Chamberlin, then, I recommend that you adopt "the method of multiple working hypotheses." More recently, John R. Platt (1964) extended that advice to propose that these many hypotheses should be framed as falsifiable. At this point, it is appropriate to mention the null hypothesis, that special type of falsifiable hypothesis required for statistical inference. Therefore, keep an open mind as you play one hypothesis against another. Then, as precisely as you can, write out your main questions and hypotheses.

You are now ready to work out procedures for testing your hypotheses. What shall be the design of your study? Shall it be experimental or observational, cross-sectional or longitudinal, laboratory- or field-based? Beyond that elementary decision lie a host of possible designs, amply illustrated in the literature and in textbooks of experimental designs. Yet if none of these fits the questions you seek to answer, keep in mind that what you seek to discover takes precedence over orthodoxy of design.

How often are we told to choose the simplest design (as though that were not exactly what we are trying to do) and, because no one can measure everything, to choose carefully among the possibilities? As David Shakow advised me years ago, keep your thinking complex but your measures simple, that is, definable, quantifiable, and independent, one from another—advice phrased by Jacob Cohen (1990) as "less is more" and "simple is better." Yet, as statistical procedures become ever more sophisticated, the possibility exists that meaning can be found in increasingly complex designs, as vividly illustrated by Everitt and Hay (1992).

Consulting a Statistician

In designing your study, consider seeking the help of a statistician. I do not mean help in choosing the proper statistical analysis for the data you have yet to collect (and of course, not for data you may have already collected). Rather, I am proposing a series of discussions beginning with the genesis of your idea for a study and concluding with the choice of a design that most efficiently tests its hypotheses. Whether your plan of attack is experimental or not, you can profit from a statistician's skills, from the fresh perspective these skills provide, and from the order they will bring to your thoughts.

In an early meeting, you will be asked to state the objectives of your study in quantitative terms—and the measures you plan to take to meet the objectives. In subsequent discussions about how these measures vary (as you know from your own experience or from the literature), you can be helped to determine the number of individuals who will compose your groups, a procedure that rests on a sounder basis than the usual multiples of the number of fingers on our hands or of eggs in a dozen. At the end, you will have gained a clearer picture of the quantitative dimensions of what you intend to study and will have arrived at a design that promises a decisive answer. (See the Supplement by Don W. Hayne at the end of this chapter.)

The ease with which we rely on computers to analyze data should not absolve us from understanding what the computer is supposed to be computing. A recent advertisement for a software package says that just by pressing a button, I can compute plots of interactions of a 10-factor analysis of variance with 5 between-subject variables, 5 within-subject variables, and unequal sample sizes. Perhaps I exaggerate: if not a button, just a few keystrokes, mouse clicks, and choices from menus. These user-friendly packages decrease our seeking of statistical advice at the very time that we are using more complicated techniques such as logistic regression and structural equation models. I have heard statisticians deride some of these activities as "the mindless execution of meaningless procedures." To give the lie to that accusation, we should be able to carry out, at least in concept, the computations that the computer produces. For help, ask your statistical consultant.

The Need for Replication

A final note on design: Try to leave room for replicating some of your procedures. The literature in the behavioral sciences is replete with findings that likely would not be reproduced were the studies repeated with another sample of subjects, by a different experimenter, or in a different setting; in fact, the findings might be quite different. For example, how can we arrive at general statements about the phenomenon under study from the findings on a local, available, and convenient sample, given its many sources of variability?

To test the hypotheses with samples from different geographical areas and different cultural and socioeconomic groups is scarcely possible for the individual investigator. For a consortium of scientists it would be possible, but only after much planning and with close monitoring. You, however, as that individual investigator, could study at least one other sample of the original population, if only as part of a second study, other variables being introduced in other parts. Then, if you found no statistically significant difference between the two samples, at least for that particular population you could be more confident of your findings.

THE PLAN ON PAPER AND AT TEST

As the plan takes form, you will find it helpful to write a full statement of what you propose to do. Ideas become real on paper, as they did for your doctoral proposal. In the first instance, you need a detailed plan for approval by the ethical review board, then for a grant proposal, and above all for yourself. What is the purpose of the study and why is it important? Who are the subjects, how are they selected, and how many do you need? What are the behaviors of interest and how are they recorded and measured?

Under what conditions may a record be discarded? Think through every detail so that once you start to gather data, you are not stopped in midstream by one you had overlooked. (My notes here say, "Where can the participants park their cars?") Also, mock up the form the data will eventually take.

As soon as your plan has been approved by the ethical review board, you can put it to the test. As I once noted, although one plans research in the ivory tower, one conducts it in the theater of life. Do the procedures produce the behavior of interest? Do the human participants understand and follow the directions as you worded them? Do the animals respond as you expected? Does the apparatus perform as planned? I recall building a fine experimental apparatus for chicks, only to have them settle down in an apparent stupor when placed in the narrow walled alley designed to lead them to the stimuli. But once placed on just an open board, with no barriers to sight, they moved swiftly to the stimuli. Then, however, they pecked at the base of the small glass cups containing the stimuli rather than at the stimuli themselves, a problem finally solved by using a platform with circular openings mounted directly over the cups so that only the stimuli were visible. As I write, I see an entry in my notebook for that study, dated 3 March 1954: "Above all, I came to realize, slowly and painfully, how much time and effort must be spent to learn the ways of a species different from one's own."

Once again, evaluate each planned measure. Do you have too many? Will they blur the sharpness of your main predictions? Even after many revisions, you may still encounter surprises when the data do not conform to expectation. In stirring language, Abraham Kaplan (1964) described the process: "The experimenter is active in seeking out, designing, and constructing the experimental situation, in doing the experiment, and making something of it. But he is passive in accepting the outcome whether or not it accords with his expectations. After all the planning and preparation, a time comes when the voice of the experimenter is stilled while nature speaks" (p. 155).

Here I am reminded of the students' and my efforts to see if toddlers would share objects with their parents. In one study we predicted that the children would share novel objects more often than familiar ones—but they did just the opposite. Although the effective properties of the familiar objects were not pursued in further studies (as they should have been), the results revealed a hitherto-unsuspected aspect of the familiar. As Medawar (1979) put the matter, "If an experiment does not hold out the possibility of causing one to revise one's views, it is hard to see why it should be done at all" (p. 94). We did, indeed, gain a new respect for the attribute of familiarity. How different the actual course of an investigation from the tidy and apparently logical way in which it will eventually be reported in the literature!

A MANUAL OF PROCEDURE

Once a study has begun, you will need to exert great care to see that the agreed-upon procedures are followed exactly. Heads nod, eyes glaze over, little changes slip in and escape notice, until suddenly a major revision is in effect. To ensure that deviations do not occur, compose a manual of procedure that covers every detail, from the obtaining of subjects to the analyzing and storing of the data.

To illustrate what I have in mind, I summarize the last manual we prepared for studying children's social behavior. The importance I attached to it accounts for its peremptory tone, although as I read it today, the tone does startle me. The first page stated: "This is the definitive manual of procedures. Anyone who participates in the work of the laboratory is expected to be familiar with it. Procedures may change from study to study but the guidelines set forth here will hold in the main." To remind the students and staff of the ethical standards governing our research, the second page presented the procedures for obtaining approval, together with a copy of the request and the date of its approval by the department's and university's review committees. And, to remind all of us of the confidence the outside world placed in our efforts, the next pages explained that the work of the laboratory was supported by federal and university funds.

The body of the manual detailed the procedures for obtaining participants (including a sample of the telephone call and the keeping of a log of all calls), preparing data sheets, setting up the experimental rooms and the apparatus (e.g., checking the microphones and the cameras), meeting the parents and children at the entrance to the building and escorting them to the laboratory, operating the equipment and recording the behavior, labeling and storing the data, closing down the apparatus, and cleaning the rooms. Subsequent sections presented the rules for coding behavior from the video- and audiotapes and for obtaining measures of observer-agreement.

At least a day before each subject's visit, persons were assigned to various duties, as were alternates in case of illness or some unforeseen absence. Their directions stated:

> Once a task is assigned to you, it is your responsibility to see that it is done properly. If you are rushed for time and have to ask someone to help, it is still your responsibility to see that the task is properly completed. At the same time, do not take it on yourself to do other persons' tasks without first telling them. Any inconsistency can cause confusion and ultimately the task may not be done.

To ensure that no parent's time and goodwill or any staff member's efforts would be wasted, extensive checklists were developed for setting up the experimental and apparatus rooms. The note here (written by Carol O. Eckerman in 1971, but followed for years thereafter) said, "Be formal in your use of the checklists," and instructed the person who did the tasks to check them off as done, and the checker to read them for the doer's assent. Both persons signed the lists, which were filed in the subject's folder. By these means I was sure that, for each parent and child, the toys had been washed, the electrical outlets covered, their identifying number together with the date and hour recorded on the videotape, and so on. Martinets we were, indeed!

At the least, a manual of procedure will give you the information you need to write the method section of the final report. Beyond that, it tells of your concern for standards. Above all, it shows your helpers the important part each plays in the enterprise; from mere assistants and students—it is my fond conceit—they become, to quote Sigma Xi's motto, "Companions in Zealous Research."

WEEKLY CONFERENCES

In addition to a manual of procedure, I found that weekly lab meetings, attended by students, assistants, and staff, furthered the work. Together we reviewed our progress, raised questions, and worried about how to do "it" better. The meetings gave us a sense of camaraderie and pride and, I hope, took the edge off the peremptory tone of the manual. An easy friendliness developed so that often the discussion went beyond the research in hand to new scientific findings and statistical procedures, and even relevant current events—indeed, to whatever seemed new, interesting, and challenging. For me, the meetings became a weekly delight because I was not treated as the senior professor, but as just a member of a congenial group engaged in a common enterprise. For a research group to meet regularly is not a new idea; it is a common practice everywhere. But just in case it may have slipped your mind, I recommend it to your attention.

PARTICIPATING IN YOUR RESEARCH

Who "runs" the subjects in your research—a computer, or your assistants, or do you? Obviously, so boldly stated, any answer would be unrealistic, but I state it thus to make my point—namely, that I think you have much to gain by taking an active part in your research. Despite the ads for computer programs that write most of the program for you, run the subjects, and analyze the data, I expect there still may be some room for your participation. And if you dream of an army of students and assistants out there gathering data and then bringing curves and printouts of p values to your desk, I suggest that you wait until you are prepared for unknown risks.

Instead, try to participate in every phase of the actual work: instructing human subjects or caring for animal subjects, setting up the conditions of study, using the apparatus, recording the data, and so on. Your efforts show the students and assistants that you are interested and concerned and that you regard their contributions as important. Furthermore, you can detect problems before they become serious. Perhaps the planned procedure should be modified. How should you code a behavior that does not exactly fit a previously defined category? Should some data be discarded because of some unspecified occurrence? The same problems could very well arise for your assistants, who, not wishing to bother you, might solve them by themselves in some way unknown—or worse yet, unacceptable—to you. Could you, then, in good conscience testify to the trustworthiness of your data?

Most important of all may be the new insights you gain by immersing yourself in the process of gathering data. At such a time, all your faculties are concentrated on the behavior of interest; the rest of the world fades away, and, lo and behold, you glimpse a new idea. At least, so it has happened to me, and I cannot be alone. Certainly, you do not have to do it all by yourself, but you should do enough to be familiar with every step, twist, and turn of the procedure. And above all, do not rob yourself of the opportunity to see something that no one else has noticed and that now sets the topic of your next study.

SUPPLEMENT

WHY YOU SHOULD TALK TO A STATISTICIAN EARLY

DON W. HAYNE

North Carolina State University

June 1992

There are two sound reasons for discussing the nature of your research with a statistician at the time you are starting to think about it. These two reasons can be identified as defining your scientific questions and considering sample sizes. There is the added fact that any time you can persuade an intellectual peer to think seriously about the details of your work, you likely will benefit.

Defining the scientific questions can be termed "identifying the falsifiable hypotheses," but the procedure includes much more. To allow the statistician to think about your problem, you must first describe exactly what you want to find out and how you think you can go about this research. To explain everything in sufficient detail, under questioning, you will be forced to think through the minutest point of reasoning and procedure, something you probably will find that you have not yet done for yourself. A good statistical advisor will insist that you explain every step, and, if nothing else, will force you to specify the assumptions you are making. You may, at this early stage, feel humiliated at not having explored these questions before, but the chances are that the advisor is not so much scientifically prescient as, rather, merely familiar with the restrictions imposed on scientific inquiry by the use of statistical inference.

The second question for this preliminary conference is about sample sizes that may be required. Contrary to the opinion of many investigators, exploring required sample sizes at this early stage is only responsible behavior, in that carrying through a study based on sample sizes that could have been foreseen to be inadequate wastes resources—in particular, that precious resource of the investigator's efforts. Although it may be argued that "some information is better than none," it is rare that knowledge is truly advanced by an observational study of very poor precision or a hypothesis test that finds "no significant difference" when the power of detecting a reasonable difference is very low. By determining early what numbers of samples are needed, you decide whether your resources will support the work you have in mind and, consequently, whether you should proceed.

The determination ahead of time of just what sample sizes will be necessary to provide respectable precision or respectable power of a test requires, in addition to an understanding of the proposed study design, a knowledge of the variability among like subjects at any one time, and the variability within individual subjects over time. Such knowledge of variability is rarely easy to find; the best source is your own past experience, and the next best source is the work of other investigators in the same field as reported in the literature. Deriving estimates of statistical variance from published studies will take a cooperative effort: You will find the studies and explain them to the statistician, and the latter will recalculate the required variance. This step requires a creative reconstruction of the reported statistical analysis, because the magnitude of variance is so seldom reported directly. Finally, if no reliable evidence of variance among subjects can be found, you and the advisor may be reduced to guessing ("estimating") a likely range for the variance, and examining the consequences if the true value is at either extreme of the range.

With your study design refined and with the required sample sizes known, you may now decide whether to proceed with your study as planned, seek further resources, or revise your study in light of statistical reality.

III

DEVELOPING YOUR CAREER

7

ADVANCING IN ACADEME

Books and articles advise you to set your career goals early, to plan now for "what you want to be when you grow up." I often asked that question of students when they first came by my office. I asked it with tongue in cheek, but it never failed to startle them, for they thought they were already grown up. There may indeed be some few persons (and you may be such a one) who have specific career goals, acquired early and maintained unchanged, but for many persons such goals are more often general and vague, open to growth and discoveries.

As I have observed the career paths of my students and colleagues—not to omit my own—it seems to me that careers develop just as all of us develop. Only by studying this topic or that, performing this activity or that, do you come to know how well a particular topic or activity suits your abilities and satisfies your dreams, how stimulating or how deadening it is, and how eagerly each day is anticipated. Even though scholarly and professional activities are never the same from moment to moment, nevertheless, in not too many weeks or months you will have learned a great deal about yourself in relation to the activity and will have come closer to defining your goals for the near, but not yet the farther, future.

In the meantime, the world does not stand still. Momentous events occur that change our view of life, the world, and ourselves. Discoveries are made, new theories are proposed, and disciplines coalesce and break asunder. A course taken, a book read, a play seen, a sermon heard—how could they not affect our thinking and our goals? Outside our work, our personal lives also change, and the needs and wishes of the people we love, of those we rear and take care of, may well alter our professional goals. And, all the while, we are growing older, surviving the slings and arrows of fortune, repressing disappointments, while cherishing rewards and honors. That is how careers develop. Advancing through the ranks in an institution of higher learning is only one of the many ways they develop. (At the end of this chapter, James O. Freedman [Supplement 1] portrays the full flowering of an academic career, and William H. Redd [Supplement 2] describes a career in a research institution.)

To return to your career, your first years as an assistant professor go fast and leave little time for thinking about the future. But now that you are reasonably well settled—your environment at home and at school more familiar, your teaching a bit smoother, your dissertation more or less ready for submitting to a journal, and perhaps a research plan in mind—it is time to consider what lies ahead. Indeed, before the next year is out, your department will be weighing your talents and achievements in terms of the formal stages of advancement. What are the stages, who decides, and on what are the decisions based? The process of advancing is carefully orchestrated and painstakingly deliberated under the watchful eye of the AAUP, whose policies and regulations are adopted by our institutions of higher learning. For you, of course, the next stage is associate professor and the usually concurrent granting of tenure.

THE FACULTY RANKS IN OPERATION

Throughout the country, agreement prevails on the distinction between tenure-track and nontenure-track positions and, for a tenure-track position, on the length of the probationary period and the timing of decisions for reappointment, promotion, and tenure. In general, as an assistant professor you are considered to be on probation for a period not to exceed 7 years. You will be evaluated periodically during that period and in greater depth at the end of 6 years, a process that leaves a year for planning if you are not to be promoted. Then, after several years as an associate professor, you are considered for promotion to full professor. There are, however, some variants and alternatives, and any special standards adopted by your department or school would be brought to your attention.

The policies and regulations are so precisely fixed that on first thought one may question how to reconcile that fact with the much-vaunted freedom of a professor's life. I reason the answer thus: The policies and regulations protect your academic freedom and at the same time ensure that at regular intervals you will be considered for advancement.

The central actors in the review process are persons in your own department—the head and the senior professors; it is they who initiate requests for appointment and promotion. Assembled, they consider your record deliberately and conscientiously. (Here again, I call your attention to how much the members of the faculty control the fate and future development of candidates, and hence of their own department and institution.) A vote is taken and sent to the dean, who may, depending on the institution's procedures, consult a specially appointed committee. The department has worked hard to reach a decision and does not take kindly to having it reversed, and it seldom is. On rare occasions, however, some larger issue of financial exigency or major reorganization may override the department's wishes. Eventually the decision is referred pro forma to the trustees, or similar officers, who alone have the legal power to appoint, reappoint, promote, or grant tenure.

What are the criteria on which the decision is based? Be prepared for the torrent of abstract nouns I find in various publications: teaching effectiveness; distinguished scholarly achievements; independent, original, and significant research contributions; institutional usefulness; academic leadership; collegial responsibility; and personal qualities of integrity, self-reliance, and tolerance! No document I have examined prescribes any fixed weighting of a candidate's relative strengths in these various traits, nor any fixed scale of criteria for any single rank. Not only are all special to the candidate, but every department and institution forever aspires to improve its academic standing.

In general, however, three major areas of your activity are evaluated: scholarly and research productivity, teaching, and service. (Let it be noted that the absolutely essential traits of personal integrity, self-reliance, and tolerance fall outside these categories; but see "Integrity as a Faculty Member" [Supplement] by Lyle V. Jones, in chapter 12.) Of these, scholarly and research productivity would seem to be the easiest to measure. One could of course just count the number of papers read at meetings and the number published, but the judges are more knowledgeable than that. In my experience, they earnestly try to gauge the quality of the articles and research reports as well as the reputation of the journals in which they are published (indeed, it may surprise you to know that the production of *too many* publications arouses doubts). Also in this category goes evidence of grants applied for and approved. Today, the emphasis on research in tenure evaluation is being criticized. We bandy about the phrase "publish or perish"—to the amusement of the cartoonist who drew a tombstone on which was carved the epitaph "He Published and He Perished," and the derision of Jacques Barzun, who wrote that we are all perishing of publishing. The emphasis is cited, unfortunately and I hope inaccurately, as the putative cause of careless research and, more seriously and I believe questionably, as detrimental to teaching.

I place teaching second only because it seems more difficult to evaluate, even though it has to be the quintessential activity of a professor in any institution of higher learning, and one that carries even greater weight in many 4-year liberal arts colleges. Any evaluation first takes into account the number of classes a professor meets, their level (whether elementary or advanced), and their size; this information shows how heavy a "load" the candidate carries, as well as the students' demand for the classes. Then the review committee can examine course outlines and other teaching materials, seek the judgment of colleagues, and formally and informally canvass student opinion.

The third area of activity, service, refers to service to your institution. In the large sense, service to the world outside the campus is also viewed as service to the institution. In the narrower sense, it includes honoring the institution's customs and ceremonies, and serving on the committees that further the faculty's academic and professional goals.

Last, the department requests letters of appraisal from knowledgeable persons outside the institution—persons of reputation in your area—some suggested by you and some chosen by the department.

SATISFYING THE CRITERIA

Once again, I go back to where I left you at the end of your first years as an assistant professor. So little time to prove yourself again! Yet worry you must, because formal reviews of your progress are already being planned, with promotion to associate professor and the granting of tenure as the end in view. (On my campus, the first of the periodic reviews—whether you are to serve out the probationary period—would be coming up soon.) To blunt any resentment you may feel at the relatively short time you are given, think ahead to the advantages of promotion and tenure: the guarantee of academic freedom, the chance to pursue your work without interruption for the next few years, and an increase in salary that will help you realize some personal dreams. Consider, also, that periodic reviews mean you are not being consigned to languish for years in your first rank. Still, a paying position for life is scarcely in your mind, nor should it be.

As a first step, review the terms of the contract you signed when you were hired, and study the policies and regulations governing academic tenure set forth in your school's faculty handbook. Next, consider afresh the mission of your institution. What are its values? Of course, they will come as no surprise; you accepted a position there because of some congruence between them and your own. Yet now you must gain so deep an understanding of them that you see very clearly the criteria on which your promotion will depend—the particular mix of teaching, scholarship, research, collegiality, and service to school and community. Then, if you have found the position to your liking, the environment pleasant, the students alert and hardworking, your colleagues congenial, and the chairperson helpful, turn your efforts to satisfying the criteria.

First, regard the head of your department as your friend and mentor, someone you often consult about your plans, dreams, problems, and difficulties, to the end that this important person may come to know you. The same goes for the senior professors in your department. Do not misunderstand me: I am not saying to insinuate yourself in a pushy manner, but rather to become known—for your strengths as well as your weaknesses.

Next, subject your teaching to as stringent an examination as you are capable of. Study the student evaluations (your superiors will!) and work toward strengthening any weakness. Keep informed of new findings in your field to keep your teaching up-to-date. Do not be ashamed to pore over the many good books on teaching; a single tip can light a fire. Consult any office on campus devoted to improving teaching, and try to attend such workshops at professional meetings. It is a truism that good teachers work to become better. So, even if you gather that on your campus, research productivity or scholarly publications are more highly valued than teaching, nevertheless know that good teaching is a sine qua non on every campus; and, if teaching is valued above all else, exert even greater effort.

The conscientious advising of students I subsume under the category of teaching. Be easily available; keep appointments with them; and extend your concern beyond the courses you teach to their growth as scholars and their development as human beings.

If you gather that research is much valued, be harshly realistic in planning what you can accomplish in the next 3 or 4 years. Play with research proposals in your mind and sketch them on paper. Be bold enough to claim a topic for your own. Originality and creativity are prized, and so also is independence. As you review the drafts of your proposals, question the wisdom of embarking on longitudinal designs—this early in your career you do not have that much time—or collaborative research, where your efforts are dependent on, and risk being delayed by, those of others. Be mindful, too, of the price one pays for multiple authorship: You will be credited only for what and how much you contributed to the work. Warnings aside, let your imagination soar, and it may come to pass that you catch a vision of an organized "program" of research.

Your next task is to think about support and services for carrying out your plans. Canvass your department and school, and then go beyond to the granting agencies, many of which have awards specially designed for untenured faculty. Discuss your ideas with interested faculty members and heed their advice. Some of these professors may participate in the decision to grant you tenure and will now be better informed. Be assiduous in pursuing your ideas, to the end of submitting an abstract of a scholarly paper or research study to one of your societies for its next meeting. Before that, seek every opportunity to present your work at small and local gatherings, and at the same time send preliminary drafts to friends and your former professors, all with the end in view of putting your ideas to the test.

Consider also the possibility of spending a summer in the laboratory of a respected investigator in your field to exchange ideas, refine your own, and try out new methods. Various agencies offer financial support for this purpose, but, of course, leaving office and home is never easy. Similarly, attending the meetings of learned and professional societies introduces you to the leaders and colleagues in your field. Here, too, travel expenses can be applied for, especially if you are presenting your own work.

Choose wisely among these possibilities. I hope you will not accuse me of being calculating when I say that some activities count for more than others in the minds of your particular evaluators and that others are better saved for later. If research is highly valued at your institution, submit your manuscript to a refereed journal; generally, the writing of invited chapters and of book reviews is less highly valued in such institutions, although highly prized in others. Overall, what counts most is the quality of your ideas, and then the industry and care with which you pursue them.

As for serving on committees and engaging in community activities, be prudent in accepting assignments. Work hard on a few rather than casually on several, while realizing that such service cannot compensate for careless teaching or scanted scholarship.

As you come to the end of the probationary period, you may be asked to prepare a record of your activities since you were hired—courses taught year by year, number of students advised, senior theses supervised, research in progress, grant proposals submitted, awards and invitations, scholarly papers written and read, conferences attended, committees, and so on. In any case, begin to assemble such a portfolio now; you will find it more impressive than you had imagined.

Materialistic as I may have seemed up to this point, I am not asking you to plot but to plan. At the same time, I advise you not to compromise your principles but to hew to your own standard of excellence.

AFTER THE DECISION

If you are promoted, heave a sigh of relief (you will, even if you were confident of the outcome), celebrate, but pause only briefly. You are entering a period in your life when you are capable of great energy and creativity. Capitalize on the momentum of the past few years. If you could accomplish so much in a few years, what more can you not in the years ahead? (Of course, you have a personal life, and you have somehow to bring that life and your professional life into a single harmonious existence. I don't bring the problem up everywhere it has a bearing, but let no one think I am not acutely aware of it.) To keep you striving, the next hurdle—promotion to full professor—lies not too many years hence. By then, however, you will have observed the process as experienced by many of your colleagues and will have learned that the process is similar but the criteria more stringent. As illustration, one department's (rather intimidating) statement reads, "To qualify for full professor, one must attain international stature in one's area of scholarship and exhibit evidence of competence in teaching, graduate training, and professional service." As for teaching, an AAUP document (1990c) proposes, in part, "Evidence of the ability to shape new courses, to reach different levels and kinds of students, to develop effective teaching strategies, and to contribute to the effectiveness of the individual's and the institution's instruction in other ways than in the classroom" (p. 168).

But what if the department decides that you are not to be promoted and that your appointment will end in another year? Some candidates anticipate this decision, ask that they not be considered, and resign before the decision, not wanting to experience the formal sign of failure. If you believe that you deserved promotion and were unfairly denied it, however, you can appeal the decision to your institution's grievance committee. In any case, stop to consider that many an outstanding scholar now at a well-respected institution was earlier denied tenure at another. Tenure decisions are particular to the time, the institution, and the candidate, and seldom does a negative decision spell the end of an academic career. Turn to your mentors for advice, study the advertisements, and apply for the next advertised opening in your field.

SUPPLEMENT 1

THE PROFESSOR'S LIFE

JAMES O. FREEDMAN

Someone has accurately defined a university president as a person who shuttles between God and Mammon. In the course of my own efforts to preach the hallowed ideals of the university while seeking the financial means of bringing them into reality, I am continually struck by the contrast between what those outside the university believe that professors do and what they do in fact.

Viewed from outside academe, the life of a university professor seems sheltered from everyday reality, a haven for those too delicate and sensitive to succeed in the workaday world. Few understand that the life of a professor is a difficult, lonely, and dedicated one. It is a life of privilege, to be sure— of autonomy in the classroom, of control over the use of time, of free inquiry, of tenure. But for those privileges, a professor pays exacting costs, in ways that are rarely visible to people who are not academics.

The first of those costs is the continuous struggle to learn afresh what remains fundamental about a discipline that is always evolving, while bringing that knowledge to life in the minds of new students.

One of the themes of Carl Sandburg's autobiography, *Always the Young Strangers*, is the renewal of society in every generation by the emergence of "young strangers"—young people who have the ability to lead their contemporaries to renew the values that sustain our culture. In the course of a semester, professors have only so many opportunities to reach those young strangers. A carelessly read term paper, a poorly conceived assignment, a flatly delivered lecture—any shortcoming in our instruction—

James O. Freedman has been president of Dartmouth College since 1987; at the time he wrote this essay, he was president of the University of Iowa. From "The Professor's Life" by James O. Freedman, 1986, *The Chronicle of Higher Education*, 31, 92. Copyright 1986 by The Chronicle of Higher Education. Reprinted by permission.

wastes an opportunity and violates our contract with those impressionable young strangers. That is why we must work for so many hours on courses we are teaching for the second, third, or even the twentieth time.

A second cost is the struggle to compress a host of protean and unruly tasks into a day that is always too short. A professor's enormous flexibility in the use of time, so incomprehensible to people who are not academics, is undeniably a great privilege, but it is purchased at a price. In the absence of a clear boundary separating vocation from avocation, teaching from scholarship, creative effort from routine chores, no single block of time can be protected from conflicting but equally legitimate demands.

Consider the quandary created by three unscheduled hours between classes on a given afternoon. Should a conscientious professor spend those hours refining the next classroom presentation, checking on new library acquisitions, catching up with reading in professional journals, doing research for a new article, double-checking a dubious experimental result, drafting a committee report, conferring with students who need extra attention, writing letters of recommendation, preparing a budget for a grant application, or revising the syllabus for next semester's course? Indeed, those golden unscheduled hours, so apparently free in prospect, are in actuality already oversubscribed before the day begins.

A third cost—one that can never be paid in full—is the responsibility to create new knowledge, whether in the library, the laboratory, or the studio. Because the search for knowledge is open-ended, there can be no point of conscientious rest.

During the unending struggle to make sense of the unknown, the scholar's identity hangs always in the balance. When a professor confronts the emptiness of the unwritten page, the silence of the laboratory instrument, the blankness of the computer screen, all certainties evaporate. The identity of the true scholar, no matter how much he or she has already achieved, is always at risk. The next book, the next poem, the next scientific finding, the next work of art may never come—or so it seems when the capricious muse of scholarship has departed, leaving only the gathering fear that it will never return.

A fourth cost is the obligation to repay society's heavy investment in the protection of independent thought. This obligation rests upon perhaps the least understood of all the privileges of a professor's life, the protection provided by tenure.

Outside of academe, tenure is frequently misunderstood as conferring a sinecure. But tenure has nothing to do with job security in the ordinary sense. Its primary purpose is to serve society's need for independent criticism and a continuous flow of new ideas. The creation of knowledge is inherently threatening to the existing order. It disrupts the pieties of a settled past, the complacencies of a comfortable present, and the prognostications of an assumed future. That is why the search for knowledge is so closely controlled in so many other societies. And that is why, in a free society, tenure is so important.

Tenured scholars are free to choose topics for research, without regard to political or economic pressure. They are free to persist in investigations that may require an extended period of gestation before they bear fruit. They are free to explore new and unconventional areas of inquiry without the pressure of having to reach conclusions prematurely. They are free even to bite the hand that feeds them, by criticizing the very institutions upon which their intellectual and financial security depends. In the end, tenure serves the best interests of society by guaranteeing some of the most promising minds of every generation an unhurried opportunity, free from external constraints and the intellectual fashions of the moment, to investigate fundamental human concerns.

In return for the extraordinary privilege of tenure, much is expected. As mature scholars, professors have a clear obligation to fulfill the promise held out by their early achievements. They have a responsibility to press toward the frontiers of what is already understood, if only by a handful of specialists, in order to enlarge what the rest of us know. They have an obligation to raise hard questions, take unpopular positions, and accept intellectual risks—in short, to build up a significant body of excellent work that opens new horizons for their successors.

But just as the costs of a life of scholarship and teaching are largely invisible outside the academic community, so are its unique rewards.

The reward that animates every scholar is the joy of discovery—the satisfaction of finding out what no one else knows and of making that knowledge available to others. At the heart of that joy is the sublime delight in getting something absolutely, unmistakably *right*. That is the joy that laboratory scientists feel when they devise an experiment that not only works the first time but that can also be flawlessly replicated and verified by others. That is joy that mathematicians feel when they know that their colleagues will recognize their theorems and proofs as "elegant." That is joy that essayists feel when they liberate an idea from the modish jargon of a single discipline and offer it to the larger community of students and scholars.

Surely, a scholar's most substantial reward is what Oliver Wendell Holmes, Jr., called "the secret isolated joy of the thinker, who knows that, a hundred years after he is dead and forgotten, men who have never heard of him will be moving to the measure of this thought. . . ." Holmes called that satisfaction "the subtle rapture of a postponed power." At the close of long days of work, at the conclusion of long years of scholarly solitude, professors are entitled to feel that rapture, to recognize that their teaching will create a ripple of influence that will be felt in the lives of students years after graduation. They need to be reassured that although their scholarship may appear in obscure journals and be read by perhaps only twenty or thirty of their colleagues today, it may set an agenda for research that will shape a discipline for years to come. They need to be reminded that future generations will indeed move to the measure of their thought.

But professors, like all others whose identity is closely tied to their professional achievements, also need immediate and tangible gratification.

In a period of intensified competition for limited financial resources, professors as well as presidents must understand that academic excellence is not only its own reward but also the key that unlocks the coffers of Mammon. And presidents as well as professors must understand that the measure of the scholar's thought is the source of a university's vitality and the standard by which it must judge itself. Nothing else, not even the most lavish favors granted by Mammon, has value except as a means to that end.

SUPPLEMENT 2

A CAREER WITHIN A RESEARCH INSTITUTION

WILLIAM H. REDD

Memorial Sloan-Kettering Cancer Center

November 1991

The domain of psychology is broad and we are fortunate to have many career choices. The purpose of this discussion is to examine some critical issues for a psychologist engaged in full-time research within a research institution. To provide a perspective on my comments, I will first describe my background, identify my point of view, and explain why I work with a research institution. I will then address what I believe to be the major issues. There are five: academic freedom, intellectual stimulation, membership on a research team, research funding, and professional identity. I will end by outlining the issues that I see emerging in the future.

My observations are based on a 23-year career working in three large medical centers and in one major university. Although my graduate training was in experimental and developmental psychology, I would be hard put to identify myself as either an experimental or a developmental psychologist. At times I have called myself a behavioral psychologist, but I often question the value of that label, as I find it difficult to determine a precise distinction between cognitive and behavioral psychology. I am a psychologist who is engaged in empirical research.

Twelve years of my career were happily spent as a university professor in a psychology department. However, as my research interest developed in the area of behavioral medicine, I became increasingly interested in full-time research and considerably less interested in undergraduate teaching.

Another reason for my mid-career shift was the difficulty I experienced in obtaining adequate numbers of research participants (i.e., individuals being treated for cancer) as a university professor outside a medical center.

After 8 years as a research professor in a medical research institution, I can identify two clear advantages to such a setting. First, there are fewer distractions for you and for your immediate collaborators. For example, in a research institution, your students (e.g., postdoctoral research fellows and research associates) do not have to juggle classes, teaching, and degree requirements; they are therefore able to devote greater attention to research. Second, it has been my experience that collaboration among investigators is more central in a research institution than in a traditional university psychology department. This fact is important because I find nothing more stimulating and educational than working with a group of colleagues to design a study. If your primary professional goal is to do research, then it seems to me that a research institution is the best setting.

A major issue for any scholar is the ability to pursue your own interests without interference. This issue is more relevant in a research institution, where there is likely to be a clear institutional research focus or mission. In most cases, the institution is established to pursue certain research questions. To the extent that your interests are consistent with the mission of the institution, you will be able to pursue your work with full support. If the research institution is an endowed think tank, then your options are almost limitless. If, at the other end of the continuum, the research institution is supported by industry, then your options are likely to be limited. Although this limitation is understandable, it can mean that you may have to be prepared to relocate if your interests radically shift. The university setting does not pose such a potential problem.

A related issue is the ability to engage in professional activities beyond formal research. Fortunately, this issue is generally not a problem at a research institution. Participation on national committees is encouraged and, in most cases, expected. Teaching is usually encouraged as well. It can be in the form of supervising postdoctoral research fellows, participating in institute seminars, or offering formal courses at local universities. Usually there are more opportunities to teach than can practically be enjoyed. Moreover, it has been my experience that graduate students are eager to work on a research team at a research institution because many of them find the work exciting and compelling. As your work becomes better known, the number of interested students grows quickly. Indeed, you should not worry about forfeiting the opportunity to teach by working as a full-time researcher.

Perhaps the most enjoyable aspect of working in a research institute is being a part of a research team. Depending on the particular setting, the group is usually composed of students and experienced investigators from different disciplines. In addition to formal research meetings, you meet with your colleagues individually to plan particular studies and to prepare manuscripts. For me, such a setting provides the greatest opportunity to learn, as I can be challenged from many levels. The presence of colleagues with different professional and scholarly experience makes for rich and lively interchange. For example, depending on the particular study, our team of collaborators might include an immunologist, a psychiatrist, a biostatistician, oncologists, and a psychologist; our corporate research experience ranges from 2 months (a new research assistant with a BA) to 22 years (me). It has been my experience that a research team at a university is usually narrower in composition—typically, the professor and graduate and undergraduate students.

To ensure a high level of intellectual interchange, we have established a structure of seminars and research conferences. We hold a weekly research meeting to review data and to present ideas for new studies. A separate journal club meets each week to review professional articles that are relevant to our joint work or are of particular interest to one of the members. We also attend research presentations sponsored by other departments of the institution, and colloquia at local universities. Each of us regularly attends national conferences sponsored by our respective disciplines.

Critical to the quality of professional life of our team is how we handle issues concerning recognition and competition, issues that are especially important in a research institution where much of the work is collaborative and authorships are usually shared. As the senior member of the team, I want to make sure that every person, regardless of rank, has the opportunity to contribute in ways that are most in keeping with that person's talents, and also that each contribution is recognized. To achieve these goals, we openly discuss the role of each member in each new study that is proposed. We maintain what we call a "living memo," which outlines each question that we are studying, the proposed research design, the specific responsibilities of each member, and the order of authors in the resulting reports and publications. To some, this procedure might sound overly formal and indicative of a highly competitive environment. However, I would argue it provides a structure that ensures the fair treatment of all parties.

A vital issue is research funding. Depending on the institution, all funds may have to come from outside sources. In other words, you may be on soft money. Fortunately, most institutions provide core support and funds for the salaries of the primary investigators. Nevertheless, the team must raise most of its own funds and then manage them. In order to do so, the researchers must be able to sell their research ideas to a funding agency or benefactor and demonstrate that they can effectively manage finances, supervise a group of people, and generate information of value to the academic community. Indeed, the investigator is managing a small business whose product is knowledge.

The preparation of grant applications is an essential skill for all researchers who want to survive, regardless of the setting. Of course, the foundation of a good proposal is a good idea. It is my experience that good ideas come most easily when collaboration is open and all participants take full responsibility for their assigned tasks. Our research team does its most creative and satisfying work at the time of grant writing. Unfortunately, I cannot fully explain why this is the case. There appears to be an intensity that sparks creativity: We are drawn together for a common goal, and we have a deadline to meet.

Beyond the need to have good ideas, a number of strategic issues must be considered. First, the purpose of the actual application is to convince the reviewer that the proposed plan of research will yield clear answers to important questions: The questions must be compelling; the proposal must be clearly written so that even a reviewer who is not familiar with the research topic will realize that the questions are important; and the rationale for the research design must be clear and logical. Second, the application must be reader-friendly. The best way to achieve that goal is to make certain that the proposal is well written: The organization must be clear and explicitly stated at the outset of the application. Third, the writers should anticipate possible criticisms of the research methodology and address them in the application proper; in other words, they should be on the offense. Fourth, it is essential that pilot data be presented to demonstrate that the proposed research really can be carried out. The reviewer should be provided concrete evidence of the feasibility of the research plan. Fifth, because applications are often initially approved but not funded, they should be revised and resubmitted. In preparing a resubmission, consider carefully all the criticisms raised by the review panel and directly address them in the revised application. Look at the panel's criticisms as valuable feedback and use them constructively. The reviewers have given you something very valuable—their research ideas. Similarly, if a site visit is scheduled, use it as an opportunity to obtain valuable constructive feedback on the proposal. Finally, ask your experienced colleagues to review a proposal before it is submitted.

One problem that is often encountered by psychologists working in a research institution is the loss of professional identity. In an academic psychology department, you have many role models and a large group of similarly trained colleagues; in a research institute, on the other hand, you are often a small minority, and you can quickly become isolated from other areas of psychology. This fact, plus the emergence of many specialties within psychology, often results in your missing advances in other areas of our discipline. You soon realize that you are an expert in one small area of psychology, yet grossly uninformed in many other areas. Although we would all like to think that we keep up with the broad psychological literature, it is especially difficult in a research institute; we have little time for reading, and we do not have the natural interchange with psychological colleagues outside our specialty. But there is a silver lining: Thanks to the considerable flexibility that characterizes most research institutions, the psychologist often has the opportunity to define a new role.

I am quite optimistic regarding the future for the psychologist interested in a career as a full-time researcher. Depending on the research area, there is increasing demand for individuals who are able to carry out well-designed psychological and behavioral research. An interesting example is recent congressional legislation requiring that all comprehensive cancer centers (a formal funding designation of the National Institutes of Health [NIH]) must have a behavior research unit as an integral part of their program. Since this requirement affects funding, the centers have begun active campaigns to recruit research psychologists. I predict similar requirements in other areas of medicine. However, it is important to point out that this demand for psychologists engaged in full-time research may be quite focused. As has always been the case, the more applied your area, the more opportunities you have. The future for those interested in more basic research may not be as clear. Fortunately, the applied relevance for many areas of developmental psychology is easy to demonstrate.

I would like to end by noting that I believe that the key to the past and future success of those interested in psychological research is their commitment to scientific inquiry (i.e., experimental research methods, empirical measurement of all variables, etc.). A researcher with a strong foundation in experimental methods can tackle new questions and be assured of achieving meaningful results.

8

WOMEN AND MINORITY PERSONS

Up to this point I have made no distinction by gender, race, or any other such characteristics in the advice I have offered in chapter after chapter—not in regard to preparing, teaching, or research, nor in how to read a book or how to design an elegant study, nor yet in how to treat students with compassion or research subjects with dignity. But now I think it is appropriate to consider the problems encountered by women and minorities—to outline current remedies, to weigh some of their ambiguities, and to make some recommendations—with full knowledge that I cannot do justice to problems of such deep human significance.

At the outset, let me discuss the title of this chapter. In some respects, women and minorities make strange bedfellows: Women are a majority of the adult population, and half or more of all minorities are women. Minorities, for their part, are composed of groups that differ by race (now a social and not a scientific distinction), color, religion, ethnic group, national origin, sexual orientation, physical ability, and so on. Moreover, Hispanics can be of any race, and the status of a given minority on any campus will vary by geographical location. Nevertheless, the chapter's title, even though it lumps together people of different biological traits and experiences, is favored for its conventional use and, what is more, for the number of problems women and minorities hold, and have held, in common.

THE PROBLEM

Both women and minorities are underrepresented in the halls of higher learning. Although women are well represented in graduate school, and especially in departments of psychology, they are not as well represented among faculty members, especially at the higher academic ranks. As for racial and ethnic minorities, they constitute smaller proportions of graduate students and especially of the faculty.

These figures have improved considerably over the past few decades and reflect an increasing sensitivity to the rights of all persons. Yet, although we can expect them to continue to improve decade by decade, that is no longer sufficient. Today, issues of stereotypical thinking and past discrimination are being swept aside to meet the shortage of professors and scientists that is predicted for the next decade. Suddenly, the number of women and minorities in academia must increase—to advance those already in place and to bring up the next cadre. We cannot afford to overlook the formerly invisible.

SOLVING THE PROBLEM

I propose a direct, personal, and withal powerful plan, one that enlists the efforts of those who are already members of academia. The process begins in the classroom with professors who work to spark the interest of women and minority undergraduates in scholarly and research activities, who encourage them to pursue graduate study, who work diligently to improve their academic performance, and who bring professional opportunities to their attention. And the process does not end with that first letter of recommendation, because there should always be more letters to come as these protégés advance. Stimulating, encouraging, and urging each such person now becomes (as it should always have been) the duty of every established professional.

At a more general level, various campus committees are working to increase the representation of women and minorities. Close to students and professors are faculty committees that oversee such matters as the admitting of students and the hiring and promoting of faculty members. At a remove, many professional and learned societies have similar committees. For example, the AAUP has a Committee on the Status of Minorities in the Profession and another on the Status of Women in the Academic Profession, and the American Institute of Biological Sciences recently urged its constituent societies to increase their efforts to support their women and minority members.

Closer to home, the APA has a full-time staff to deal with issues of women and minorities. The APA's Office of Ethnic Minority Affairs publishes *The Directory of Ethnic Minority Professionals in Psychology* (1990) to help recruit and advance minority persons. The association also publishes *Toward Ethnic Diversification in Psychology Education and Training* (Stricker et al., 1990) to alert its membership to the needs of minorities. In 1992, APA's Committee on Women in Psychology published *Survival Guide to Academia for Women and Ethnic Minorities*. Earlier, in 1988, the committee published the third edition of *Understanding the Manuscript Review Process: Increasing the Participation of Women*, a brochure that exhorted women to persist in submitting manuscripts in the face of the to-be-expected initial rejection. (Good advice for everyone!) These committees hold conferences, workshops, and symposia and report on them in our journals and newsletters. They have their constituents' welfare at heart, and from their efforts, women and minority persons can draw a measure of confidence.

Beyond the good offices of these committees are funds provided by public and private agencies to support underrepresented persons. The National Science Foundation (NSF) and the NIH offer a multitude of awards to support the training and research of women and minorities. Some awards are for established scholars, some for those not yet established, and some for those returning to school after an absence. Furthermore, investigators already holding grants from NIH can obtain additional supplementary funds to add minority students to their projects, and NIH will also help to improve the libraries and laboratories of institutions with many minority students. Private foundations, too, have special programs for women and minorities, some of them supporting leaves for scholarly activities.

The most important of these many efforts to increase the number of underrepresented groups have been in place for many years. Title VII of the Civil Rights Act of 1964 prohibits discrimination in employment, and Executive Order No. 11375 of 1967 mandates special efforts to recruit, employ, and promote qualified members of underrepresented groups. Virtually every institution of higher learning has an affirmative action plan, and an affirmative action office to oversee all appointments and promotions. For every faculty opening, a department must report where and for how long the position was advertised, the gender and race of all applicants, and the reasons for excluding any female or minority person from consideration.

Advertisements for professors, postdoctoral fellows, and the like in the *Monitor*, the *APS Observer*, *Science*, and the *Chronicle of Higher Education* vividly illustrate efforts to increase the number of women and minority members in academe. Institution after institution declares itself an "equal opportunity employer" and a supporter of affirmative action. Many add that they are "particularly interested in receiving applications from women and minorities" or that "applications from multicultural and women candidates, including individuals with disabilities, are especially encouraged." Here in these ads we see the culmination of the good offices of individuals, committees, and granting agencies, all buttressed by the laws of the land, to meet the nation's need to increase the number of qualified persons.

ON FURTHER THOUGHT

For some time to come, issues of affirmative action will be debated. Is it truly an affirmation and not a discrimination? "Quotas, once again?" In ending old preferences are we creating new ones? Affirmative action has become a legal and political problem, not to be resolved in everyone's best interest for the near future. In the meantime, a few related issues bear examination.

Some beneficiaries of affirmative action, for example, resent preferential treatment. In particular, many women believe that affirmative action violates the meaning of equality, implying as it does that they cannot qualify by ability alone. At least two generations of women have succeeded in the professions and the sciences (no less, in psychology) without special privilege. As we serve on today's review and other advisory committees, some of my own generation (myself included) often wonder whether we were chosen to serve because of our ability or rather to fulfill some agency's newly mandated statutory obligation to include women—an unsettling thought that previously never crossed our minds. I recall, too, how not too long ago I used all my powers to persuade a Black woman graduate student applying for a faculty position to check the box, African American; she wanted to be considered on her professional competence and not the color of her skin.

Then, as there are good reasons to increase the number of women and minorities in academia, we can question the claim that women and minorities are needed to provide different points of view (the term is *diversity*). I find myself asking: Did all my male professors at the University of Chicago have identical points of view? Not at all! What a strange department of psychology that would have been! Nor did I detect a "feminine" point of view in Helen L. Koch, my only female professor. All had different views about the methods of science and the laws of behavior, but these seemed due more to individual differences than to class membership. Does the ability to teach, to be a scholar, or to conduct research differ by gender, race, or ethnicity?

The proposed advantage of diverse points of view based on gender, ethnic, or other class membership is accompanied by the assumed value of providing role models. What, indeed, are the personal characteristics our students and young professors should emulate? My own list would start with a lively and inquiring mind and a drive to teach and would end with competence and compassion undergirded by an upright character. Nowhere in my list do I see gender, color, ethnicity, and so on. Although it may be easier to imitate the behavior of someone who resembles you in these latter characteristics, they do not provide the important stuff of which role models are made. Let us, rather, choose as role models persons of stature: heroes and heroines who are acclaimed because of their abilities and virtues.

The case for diverse viewpoints and role models, then, seems not *in itself* to offer compelling reasons for adding women and minorities to the cadre of scientists and professors. In fact, such reasons may diminish the more important ones. We can uphold justice for its own sake—not for nice-sounding slogans. Given the temper of the times, it has taken courage for me to tarnish their luster.

FOR WOMEN ESPECIALLY

The unique problem for a woman is the combining of motherhood and work, of bearing children and caring for them while carrying out academic, scholarly, and professional activities. And along with the care of a family go a multitude of domestic duties. At no point in this chapter do I intend to ignore the role of men as members of minorities or to slight their contributions as husbands and fathers; but the words of Phyllis Rose (1983) apply here: "Marriage and career, family and work, which so often pull a woman in different directions, are much more likely to reinforce one another for a man" (p. 150).

Countless women have brought marriage and career, family and work into harmony, and their contributions to psychology are considerable (for a review, see Russo & Denmark, 1987). In fact, married women with children publish as much as their single female colleagues do (Cole & Luckerman, 1987). Nevertheless, combining family and work amidst a whirl of conflicting demands qualifies as one of life's great endeavors, never easy but always challenging.

Let us first consider the timing of these endeavors. Shall a woman marry and bear children and then prepare for her career, or should she first establish a foothold in academia? What should that foothold consist of— obtaining a PhD, a year or two of postdoctoral training, and a tenure-track assistant professorship? Or, may not parts of one course be interspersed with those of another? In truth, I cannot advise on the timing of these epochal events. They are individual matters, subject not even to benevolent advice; there is no "best" timing for everyone.

Some years ago, I would have advised my women students to complete their education first—not to leave the university until they had obtained the PhD—and to secure a tenure-track position as an assistant professor before they had children (a schedule I myself did not follow). This is still the choice of many women. Today, however, I sense a relaxing of the accustomed course (for men as well as for women)—a questioning of the accustomed progression and a readiness on the part of universities and colleges to accommodate the changes.

Many forces seem to be at work here. Students drop out to earn money, to gain work experience, or to have children, and then return. Older people are returning to school for graduate and postgraduate study. At the same time, established persons also move about: They take scholarly leaves to read, think, and write; they learn new skills, change areas of interest, and collaborate on interdisciplinary projects.

These trends toward flexibility favor the needs of women, and they ease transitions between home and campus. Child care can combine with part-time study and part-time work, and the woman who returns to school after an interruption finds company among her classmates. More and more often, maternity (and family) leave policies modify teaching schedules and extend the time for tenure decisions, and more and more institutions provide child care on campus. Are these special privileges? Yes, and some women will have none of them, and push through to success without sacrificing children or work. Only a few years ago, in a first draft on this topic, I wrote, "Because one is a woman, no quarter should be asked, none should be expected, and none accepted." Now I have mellowed, and I come down on the side of a woman's need for more time: time to reach the level of competency she aims for, and time to fulfill her aspirations for both family and career. We grow on all kinds of experiences, and motherhood rates as a rare experience.

I end this section with a tribute to Professor Gillian Cell, a wife and mother of three children, who is now provost at Lafayette College in Easton, Pennsylvania. At UNC at Chapel Hill, she was the first woman dean of the College of Arts and Sciences; before that, she was the first woman to earn tenure in the History Department, and she became its first woman chair. In a 1986 interview with the student newspaper, Dean Cell said that she didn't see herself in a pioneer's role: "That really gets tiring. I happen to be a woman, and I happen to do this job. What I'd really like to see is that it not even be a cause for comment" (Fleischer, 1986).

MEETING THE CHALLENGE

If you are a member of any underrepresented group, I advise you to find a mentor directly—advice that holds for men as well as for women. Choose someone who seems interested in what you are interested in, someone always ready to talk to you and to answer your questions thoughtfully and at length, someone who is not only willing to read your papers but also (and this is a great deal more important) self-confident enough to criticize them honestly (nothing is less helpful than just a "Good" or "Interesting" scribbled in the right-hand corner of the first page). Your mentor can be male or female, of any color, ethnic, or religious background, rural or urban, Ivy League or not; encouragement and good advice are not the preserve of only your equal number. I recall how throughout my own professional life I was buoyed up by David Shakow's interest and genuine delight in my work. At the same time, try to find someone whom *you* can encourage and advise. Let that person be someone of either gender, of any race or background. Just as a mentor can enrich your life, so can you enrich someone else's. In helping another, you are helped—and of all I have to say in this section, this is my best piece of advice.

Next, tap the resources designed especially for you. Opportunities abound for fellowships, research grants, and scholarly leaves. For example, a recent issue of *Science* announced a workshop for minority scholars sponsored by the AAAS; the participants were to come from the following groups: Asian/Pacific Islander, Black/African American, Hispanic/Chicano/Latino, and Native American/American Indian, their expenses to be paid by the association. Many similar opportunities appear in the newsletters and journals of professional societies. Only by applying can you learn *how* to apply—and how to be successful. Know that help and support are out there somewhere, and canvass assiduously.

On occasion, hard as it may be, try to forget your membership in the underrepresented, so that you can lose, even momentarily, the awareness of yourself as a victim. Victims of prejudice too often pity themselves, see snubs where there are none, and live in a constant state of indignation—all at the price of that peace of mind from which creative impulses arise, a cost you can ill afford (sentiments echoing those of McKay [1988]).

Day by day, take confidence in knowing that your efforts rest on a bedrock of federal rules and regulations. So, too, be assured that many persons in positions of authority in your college or university have your interests at heart and are working diligently to foster them.

I end on a more difficult note, but at the same time on a more positive one because the demands it places on you have a certain favorable outcome. Here it is: Work hard and become able—so able as to make gender, race, or ethnicity irrelevant, academically and professionally. You will be working toward the day when people will be judged as individuals and not as representatives of groups. If you think about the matter, there is no alternative.

9

PLANNING THE DAY'S WORK

As I have said, professors enjoy a measure of freedom in ordering the many calls on their time. Even though the scheduling of classes is fixed, class meetings do not consume the working day, nor do all those committee meetings and appointments with students. How to organize the other hours to carry out all the other tasks presents a great challenge, as James Freedman so vividly describes (see chapter 7). Although I have never succeeded in working out a reasonably satisfactory plan, or in keeping to any plan consistently, to this day, I am still trying. Would that I could give you an outline of a day as well spent as the one Hans Selye gives us in his book, *From Dream to Discovery* (1964). By half- and quarter-hours, he accounts for "a typical day, picked at random" (actually, 26 January 1963): from arising at 4:30 AM (thinking about his research) until lights-out at 9:30 PM (thinking about his research), including, among many other activities, dictating, lab rounds, conferences, physical exercise, and geography games with his children at dinner. In contrast, at the end of this chapter I give you an atypical day, "A Day That Went Awry."

THE DIFFICULT TAKES PRIORITY

Although I set forth a plan I think worth striving for, yet on any one day, and often on many, there will be an early morning class to teach, a meeting to attend, an unexpected visitor, roads that have iced up during the night, or a child with a temperature of 102°. Plans can be changed, plans can go unfulfilled, but plans should be made, or we list with the wind.

To my way of thinking, the most important professional task of any working day is to read, to think, and to plan and write. What should you think, plan, and write about? Whatever is the most difficult that awaits you—the lecture to prepare on a new topic, the journal article to master, the book to review, the stirring introduction of a scholarly paper to compose, the data to summarize, the grant proposal to outline, or the article to referee. For morning persons, then, those are the first tasks of the day. But you know your own biological clock and will schedule that most difficult task for whenever you are most productive.

Resist the tendency to prime the working day by doing the easy jobs first—reading the newspaper and mail (or tapping into your voice-mail), signing letters, watering the plants, chatting with the professor next door. A few people do begin that way: John Steinbeck (1969) wrote a letter to his editor each day, on the left-hand pages of his notebook, to get in the mood to continue writing *East of Eden* on the right-hand pages. For most of us, however, beginning the workday with the task that comes most easily to hand sets up distracting lines of thought that intrude on the more difficult tasks awaiting attention. Even more seriously, the sense of satisfaction that comes from accomplishing the easy task allays the anxiety of having to tackle the more difficult one, the one we don't quite know how to accomplish. Having at least done *something*, we all too easily relax. Soon other distractions creep in, and once again that most difficult task is postponed for yet another day. So, although it may take 10 to 15 minutes to clear your mind and get started, they are the minutes in which to resist the impulse to pick up something easy. Then, even if you make little progress on that most difficult task, you cannot berate yourself for not having tried.

How can you avoid the distractions and ensure that you will tackle the most difficult task early on? Start the day before! Before you leave your desk, clear it of all the less-demanding tasks. Unless you are one of those rare persons who can concentrate on difficult matters in the midst of chaos, take time to sort out, throw away, organize, and file whatever you can. Plan tomorrow's schedule—classes to meet, committee meetings and seminars to attend, letters to answer, telephone calls to make—headed by that most difficult task. Leave the schedule on your cleared desk, at home or on campus, where you will see it, and only it, in the morning. A tough assignment!

What works for you, of course, may be quite different. In a related vein, I recall the late John Thibaut recommending his practice of ending a day's writing in the middle of a sentence so that on the next day he could pick up the thread of his thought at once.

A MATTER OF TIME

Once in a while, but only once in a great while, a task takes less time than we have allotted it. As I have watched my students—and myself especially—I am impressed by our inability to gauge how much time a task will take. I therefore advise you to increase the amount of time planned for any assignment by a factor of four. By not allotting enough time, we rob ourselves of a sense of accomplishment, all the more welcome because infrequent. This advice ranks high among all that I offer.

Take time, also, to be on time. Don't make the mistake of thinking that your being late shows how many more important matters you have to attend to; what it really shows is that you think you are more important than other people. How often have I seen habitual latecomers bring a sheaf of papers to a meeting and read and even make notes on them, which only compounds their discourtesy. Still others appear to make a virtue of their tardiness, expecting us to accept it as an endearing trait.

Being on time also extends to answering your mail. As you begin to acquire a reputation, the number of letters asking for information and advice becomes very large indeed. Often a single request will take hours of reading and pondering. Nevertheless, it seems proper that all should be answered as promptly and thoughtfully as possible. Furthermore, being late in submitting a promised chapter for a planned book constitutes a very serious affront not only to the editor but also to those who submitted theirs on time; many writers of chapters can tell unhappy stories of how their contributions were delayed for several years.

Sally, a character in the cartoon strip *Peanuts*, echoes my advice amusingly. She is writing "Timeliness is next to Godliness." Charlie Brown says, "I think the correct phrase is 'Cleanliness is next to Godliness'"—to which Sally responds, "What good does it do to be clean if you're late?"

We all slip. It helps to keep that factor of four in mind.

KEEPING TRACK OF YOUR DAY

We live with the idea that we used to have more time. Nor is that idea unique to our times: George Eliot, living in the 19th century, wrote enviously of Henry Fielding, who lived in the previous century, when the days were longer, "when summer afternoons were spacious, and the clock ticked slowly in the winter evenings." Nevertheless, as we acquire more responsibilities, our days do seem to grow shorter and pass faster. A favorite cartoon by Ronald Searle shows a man desperately trying to hold the days to a wall calendar as they overflow the wastebasket and swirl in the air about him. And Steinbeck (1969), in one of the daily letters to his editor, wrote: "By some chicanery, it has become Monday. You don't dare turn your back anymore" (p. 93).

One way to slow time may be to record its passage. Diaries keep track of time, and the prime reason given by the great Victorian diarists was not to live in the past but to record the present. Without diaries, our lives slip away and our work and thoughts go unrecorded. Course notes and published papers are scant substitutes. What I offer here are a few less-demanding substitutes for keeping a diary.

First, date everything you do. As you begin your career, you can scarcely believe that the pages you write today might one day be of consequence for charting the development of your thinking. You lack the imagination now, but take my advice and begin the practice directly. What should you date? Date everything: course notes and outlines, daily schedules, and reading notes; drafts of letters, talks, and articles; and new plans and thoughts. While you are working, you cannot imagine that someday you will forget what a particular notation, now so clearly etched in your mind, refers to. Yet you will—as every scholar and teacher has had cause to lament at one time or another in trying to decide why this undated sheet of paper was so carefully preserved. Indeed, in training research assistants, one of your first tasks is to teach them the absolute importance of labeling and dating as well as prominently affixing their initials to the page.

Second, consider keeping notebooks of your readings, of lectures and seminars attended, and of your thoughts, plans, and dreams, including choice quotations—all, of course, to be dated. Notes of lectures preserve the current thoughts of authorities and provide information not likely to be in print for some time. Most valuable of all are your thoughts, insights, and plans because they mark your progress in developing an idea and often form the basis of future research and writing.

In his autobiography, Clark L. Hull (1952) described in considerable detail the notes he made of books read and seminars attended, together with his own views thereof, eventually accumulating 27 volumes. He so valued his notes as stimuli to thinking that he purchased notebooks for his promising graduate students. He ruefully ended the account with these words: "Very little evidence has reached me that the practice was adopted by any of them" (p. 148). Let us hope they did use the notebooks but failed only to let him know.

THE BURDEN OF FILING

Peek into almost any professor's office on campus and you will see few bare working surfaces. Desks, tables, chairs, the tops of file cabinets, and often the floor are covered with student examinations, letters, book ads, reprints, journals, and books, all under the vigilant eye of the computer screen. Genius has its own ways and will blossom willy-nilly, and a clear desk, to be sure, may be no more than the executive's symbol. True, what seems like disarray may be so only in the eye of the beholder; to the occupant who knows the exact position of whatever is needed, it may well be order. Yet how often have I observed my colleagues (and I do not exclude myself) shuffling through pile after pile in a desperate and often futile attempt to find the letter they need this moment and that they declare they saw just yesterday. At some time, we all experience the need to bring order out of chaos. Then we spend the better part of spring break on the task, only to find ourselves in the same predicament a few weeks later.

Of course, we could spend some time at the end of each day filing what came across the desk that day. Given the amount of paper generated by just the daily mail, that is not a simple task. And given that seldom do our offices at home or on campus contain enough surfaces and filing cabinets (and who wants to "lose" in a filing cabinet the material one is sure to need tomorrow?), some ordering of these materials must be worked out. Even now, as I write, I cannot find, or imagine where to find, my notes on the quotation from George Eliot, cited above. Is it at home or in my office, and in which folder would I have filed it? Then I think longingly of Mark Weiser's (1991) envisioned "tabs," inch-scale computers that will beep to help locate mislaid papers and even open file drawers to show the desired folder.

TIME FOR CONTEMPLATION

I have left to last what is held to be the most important, yet which proves the most difficult to program in any one day: time to think. Of course, we are always thinking. But I have in mind the gaining of new ideas and the spotting of weaknesses in our old ideas. Often, such insights come as we turn away from our reading or writing, or as we carry out mundane tasks, like traveling to work, that do not completely engage our minds. If that is so, I am not confident that setting aside "time to think" will always produce great insights. Still, some quiet time cannot be amiss and might even provide some enthusiasm for planning the day's work.

SUPPLEMENT

A DAY THAT WENT AWRY

HARRIET L. RHEINGOLD

The day of 16 April 1947 dawns with an unpredicted snowstorm that already has accumulated 4 inches and shows no signs of abating. As usual, my schedule for the day has many entries: classes in the morning at Rockford College and a faculty meeting after lunch, an infant's development to assess in the afternoon at the child guidance clinic downtown, a tea at the college president's house back on campus, and a meeting at my home that evening with the students majoring in psychology to discuss their comprehensive examinations. My husband is out of town, and the boys (aged 6 and 13) would ordinarily walk a few blocks to catch the bus to school. But yesterday Arnold, the 6-year-old, brought a note from school asking parents not to send children today because of an outbreak of measles in his class. So Arnold will stay home with the housekeeper, who comes daily. Just then I begin to worry, will the roads be maneuverable? But first we have to make a trip to the attic to get our galoshes, which have already been stored for the summer, prematurely as it turns out.

Paul, my elder son, leaves at 8 AM. It is 8:30 and the housekeeper has not come, presumably delayed by the storm, but I have to give a quiz to my 9:00 class at the college 5 miles away, so Arnold will have to come with me. I have never before had to take a child with me to work, and I have a very strong aversion to so doing. [At that time in my life I thought it unprofessional: One's personal life was not to interfere with work. One took pride in being able to organize matters efficiently, and besides, household help was easier to obtain then than today. Incidentally, Rockford was a women's college; most of its professors were unmarried, and only two were mothers.]

This account is based on notes made the day after.

121

We drive through the snow without difficulty, arrive in time, and during that first class Arnold sits quietly in the back of the room. Similarly, during my 10:00 class he continues quietly drawing—but then halfway through the hour he begins to shuffle his feet. I begin to worry not only that the noise will annoy the class but even more that I have not provided well for my child. Fortunately, the next hour is free and I can spend it in my office grading papers, working over course notes, and answering mail— but Arnold becomes increasingly restless, and I run out of material to interest him. Lunch on campus is a welcome diversion. The snowstorm is abating and the wet snow begins to melt in the warm air.

At 1:00 PM we go to the faculty lounge for the faculty meeting. I ask the president if Arnold can sit in the back of the room [an embarrassing memory!]. She objects, so I leave him in the hall outside where he had said he would not stay—once there, fortunately, he settles down cheerfully. I expect a 20-minute meeting, scheduled to consider three brief elections; the topics, however, also include salaries, and the meeting goes on and on. Knowing that I have an appointment downtown at 2:30, I sit on pins and needles, I resolve to give it all up, and I wonder how an intelligent person can get herself into such a predicament.

At 2:15 I pull out of the meeting before it ends, with guilt, and drive downtown with Arnold and leave him, with even more guilt, for his first time alone at a movie theater, which has a special show of 17 Walt Disney cartoons. At the clinic, close by, the baby arrives late (which gives me time to read my mail) and tests well, but her flannel diapers shed fluff all over my best black wool suit worn for the party later in the day.

By 3:30 I am home, planning to freshen up, and find the housekeeper (there at last) deeply absorbed in the Fuller Brush salesman's display of his wares. I buy three toothbrushes to speed him on his way. A few minutes later, a hospital insurance salesman is at the door [it was a common practice of the times for salesmen to solicit business from housewives who were home during the day]; I am extra nice because so annoyed. Finally, washed and brushed, I set out for the president's home across town and, as I leave, meet Paul, who is working his paper route. I tell him to watch out for Arnold, who will catch a bus and be home at 5:00. He asks how I think Arnold can be home at 5:00 with the movie not starting until 4:00. Another blow! Had I left Arnold at the movies at 2:30, when the show didn't start until 4:00? Paul reports, furthermore, that just two other mothers, out of 24, had kept their children home from school. Only my own punctilious compliance had ruined the day!

Home again at 5:45, but with the students coming over at 7:30, I decide to take the boys out for dinner at a nearby restaurant. [Going out to eat was an unusual event in our family and, though it is difficult to understand today, a measure of pride dictated that a woman would not sacrifice a homemaker's and mother's role to the demands of a career. (Also, it was before the day of fast-food restaurants or pizza delivery!)] Entering the restaurant rather shamefacedly, I meet a family we know with children about my sons' ages and am stunned to hear the mother (a homemaker only) say, "We are eating out because, after cleaning the sink, I thought it looked too nice to fill it up again with dirty dishes." Then, indeed, I feel virtuous; so much weightier are my reasons!

Home again, and while the boys bathe and settle down in their rooms, I prepare refreshments for the students. They arrive promptly at 7:30, and we discuss the nature of comprehensive examinations, current events, and movies they like, until they leave at 11:00 PM. [A lame ending! My notes continue, "Every day isn't so bad. Forget them quickly. Guilt because I work."]

*   *   *

As I write today, 45 years later, I cannot summon up the emotions of that day, nor account for their intensity. The children were strong, able, and alert; the town and the college provided safe environments; but two parts of my life had collided! I write this account now to relieve the smugness of my advice on how to plan the day's work. Although for me it was a day that went awry, I have been informed by one of today's young working mothers that it pales by comparison with days she and her friends have known.

10

WRITING A JOURNAL ARTICLE

On page 167 of the APA *Publication Manual* (3rd ed.; 1983) the following statement appears: "Each contribution must fill a place that before was empty, and each contribution must be sturdy enough to bear the weight of contributions to come." Assuming, now, that you have a body of findings that can make such a contribution, how should you begin to write its report? O'Connor and Woodford (1975) likened the task to trying to start an old car on a frosty morning: "The would-be driver is anxious, the car is cold and reluctant, and both man and machine suffer for a while" (p. 1). Thus, although in the process of planning and conducting the research, you have already written a great deal about your idea—its history, the procedures you followed, and the results obtained—composing its report for publication requires a fresh start.

As you will discover, the form of a journal article is as fixed as a sonnet's, and the style of writing, like the sonnet's, is marked by precision, lucidity, and brevity. For both form and style, the *Manual* provides exemplary advice on every detail of preparing a manuscript and sets the standard to which we conform.

THE PRELIMINARIES

Let us start with framing the title. True, it need not be composed until the moment the manuscript leaves your desk, but because of its importance, it deserves close attention. Not only does the title tell the world what your research is about and thus determine your readers but, as you will discover, the very exercise of its framing can go a long way toward telling you, yourself, what in fact you did study.

First, the title must be short, and yet within the recommended 12 to 15 words it should capture the purpose of the research, the results, and their significance—a tall order, indeed. Then, short as the title is, it must be further compressible into the "running head" printed at the top of a journal's right-hand pages. By these words your report will be indexed for information retrieval systems. Begin, then, with a significant word or phrase, specify the organism under study, tell what was measured, and suggest its importance. Surely, the title should be informative, but if in addition it is easy to say and remember, it may capture the attention of a few more readers. This is what I think the APA *Manual* means by "A title should summarize the main idea of the paper simply and, if possible, with *style*" (italics added; p. 22).

As we carry out a study, we tend to use simple labels for convenience, but as the research proceeds, we start to compose more formal titles. Try writing some favored candidates on the blackboard where your eye can fall on them from time to time. Thus, for daily use I labeled one of our studies "Helping," a term that in the final title became "Children's Participation in the Work of Adults." You will find that working over the title sharpens the thrust of the main idea. Lest you think that I belabor the point, recall what wonders you achieve in helping your students to clarify a murky cloud of ideas just by asking for a title of their proposed research.

The second item in a report names the author(s). Who shall be your coauthors, if any, and who deserves credit for helping you? These matters are best decided early, but as cooperation and assistance may have changed during the course of a study, now is the time for a final decision. Authorship should signal scientific and professional contributions, such as formulating the problem and the design, planning the statistical analysis, interpreting the results, and putting them into words. I state the matter more simply as participating in the research from its design to the writing of the report for publication. Other so-called lesser contributions, such as gathering data, coding behavior, running statistical analyses, and designing apparatus, should be acknowledged in a note.

These distinctions are often easier to state than to make. In many cases they can be both difficult and sensitive (Bridgwater, Bornstein, & Walkenbach, 1981; Spiegel & Keith-Spiegel, 1970). On the one hand, you are not to offer coauthorship out of deference, friendship, or sympathy; on the other, you are not to ignore a rightful claim out of neglect or disregard. Authorship should be reserved, I believe (and as the public and the recipient are entitled to believe), for those whose contribution represented an investment of time, effort, knowledge, and concern equal to that of the principal investigator or investigators. Then, as scrupulous as you are in offering coauthorship, be just so generous in acknowledging the persons who assisted you, as well as the nature of their contributions.

Now one more task remains: to check that your coauthors have read the manuscript and agree to be named (and in so doing are accepting responsibility for its contents) and, similarly, that persons whose help you acknowledge also agree to being named.

The third item, the abstract, should be framed as a working statement first and its final revision postponed until the entire paper is written and polished. I will return to it later.

THE ACTUAL WRITING

Now it is time to write the report itself. As a first step, divide all your material into folders labeled Introduction, Method, Results, and Discussion. Now, difficult as it is, resist the impulse to start with page 1 of the Introduction, and instead open the folder of Results, for there is where I recommend you start. Why? As I see the matter, the results are the heart of the report: They are the outcome of the method you employed, and from them stem the conclusions; the conclusions, in turn, are weighed in the Discussion as they relate to the purpose set forth in the Introduction, a journey that carries you to the very reason for obtaining the results. Observe, then, how central in both position and substance are the results. Furthermore, having composed the Results section, you will see how easily the other parts of the paper fall into place. Consider, too, that while theories come and go, the results, together with the procedure for obtaining them, once in archival form, last forever.

By now, you have summed and averaged the data, calculated measures of dispersion, and performed the appropriate statistical tests. Now, order these findings in importance, and organize them in tables and, if appropriate, in figures. Follow the APA *Manual's* guidelines for general advice, heed Hartley's (1991) suggestions for enhancing the clarity of tables, and study Tufte's (1983, 1990) prescriptions for designing graphic displays that most tellingly reveal the answers to the questions you raised. So prepared, you are now ready to put the findings into words, writing the text around the tables and figures. Be sure to report means and variances before you give the probabilities from statistical tests of significance, and in general avoid a long series of simple declarative sentences.

Sooner or later you will hit a snag in preparing the results, and that is a good time to turn to the less demanding task of writing the Method. Long before this stage, you will have written a detailed account of who were the subjects, how they were chosen, and how the data were obtained. Here, too, you will have recorded any unforeseen problems and how you solved them. You need now only put these parts in order, remove any irrelevant material that may have crept in, and ensure that you tell what you did in sufficient detail to be reproducible by another. The main problems you will encounter are deciding on the amount of detail and ordering the information, as you cannot say everything at once. You will find that writing this section serves as a welcome respite from the other more problematic ones. Indeed, there are no surprises here; all is known.

Once the Results section is completed, you are ready to discuss what you found in relation to what you set out to find—a weaving together of the Results and the Introduction. Even though the latter has not yet received your attention, refresh your memory of the questions you set out to answer. The first sentences of the Discussion should present the answer to them in a straightforward and powerful paragraph. Then, in subsequent paragraphs, with informative headings, consider how your findings corroborate, deny, or amplify the findings, ideas, and speculations of others. You, too, may speculate, but only so far as your data permit, any set of data being but a special sample of a universe of samples. Do not permit yourself that trite and threadbare statement, "more research is needed." (More is always needed, and if you know what is required, vow to do it.) The final paragraph should be another strong statement; like the first, it will be read more often than those in between. Here, at last, you can go beyond the data to spell out the meaning of your work for theory or practice.

Now, lay the Discussion aside and turn to the Introduction. Although you likely will have composed several drafts, start again while the Discussion is fresh in your mind. In a simple, clear, and well-crafted paragraph, present the problem or question and state why it is interesting and important. Then, develop a chain of reasoning from what is known to how you intend to solve the one or answer the other. Paragraph by paragraph, present and evaluate the thinking and research of others on all facets of the topic. While you were conducting the study, you will have acquired some new ideas and have read some new references. Indeed, by now you know a great deal more than when you started the research. Even the main thrust may be different. Whereas at one time I argued that the Introduction and the Discussion should form a unified whole—after all, they are written by one person with full knowledge of both parts—I now think that there should be only some measure of agreement; the Introduction proposes, the Discussion discovers. Here indeed there is room for surprises!

Often the full meaning of a study became clear to me only as I reached this final stage: putting the period to the last sentence. (So as not to disappoint you too much, I note here that years may pass before you grasp the study's real meaning.)

COMPILING THE REFERENCES

Here you can turn away from the exacting task of writing sentences to the easier one of reviewing your original list of references. I suggest that you examine each one carefully, and even reread some. A surprise or two may await you, as on occasion they did me. For example, in searching through one of your favored references, you may find that it does not make the point you thought it did. Or, perhaps you included some references because they are always referenced in work on your topic; on a second reading you may now question their relevance. After adding some references that came to mind as the research progressed, ask yourself if you need all those references. Weigh the aptness of each, not least of your own.

I hesitate to ask you to check every detail of a reference—it seems so small-minded—but the literature is replete with errors, as I know from experience. For example, my name has been spelled variously and my initials reversed or reduced. In a chapter in a book, a study completed 20 years after I received my degree was referenced as my doctoral dissertation. And, in several instances I have found my name in a list of references but nowhere in the text. Granted, these errors are cause more for amusement than concern; still, let us give scholarship its due. Compare each of your references, not with your notes or the citations of others, but with the original document, and check that each reference in the text is included in the list and that none remains there that is not in the text.

THE ABSTRACT

It is time now to write the abstract. It is important not only because, after the title, it is the item most often read but also because abstracts are reprinted by abstract journals and distributed by information retrieval services. Because so much information must be given in so few words, writing the abstract tests your skills most severely. You must write not only succinctly but so simply that readers outside your field can grasp the significance of your work. Yet, within all these constraints, you must present the purpose of the research, the subjects and the procedures, the main results, and their meaning. And try not to end with the feeble statement, "The conclusions are discussed"; instead, having discussed them, now summarize them. From my own experience I know that you will try many versions, counting words each time, until you write that final perfect abstract.

COMING TO THE END

Although by now you are close to a good "working" draft of the manuscript, you can do still more. First, use any forum to present your study to others, starting with your students. Defending your position and answering questions can sharpen your prose and sometimes even give rise to a vivid phrase. Second, ask a colleague or two to read and criticize the manuscript (which should be in as complete and polished a form as you can compose). Ask for the severest criticism, and profit by it. Scarcely any greater satisfaction comes your way than a journal's acceptance of a manuscript just as you have written it. In any case, the fewer the criticisms the better, and none should be of carelessness.

One more word before you send the manuscript to a journal: Here and there I see advice that the best way to write the report is to start on page 1 and continue to the end, preferably in one sitting—quite different from my advice. I do appreciate the thrust of that advice; it could produce a lively, forward-moving, coherent style, and a bit of spontaneity. That counsel suggests a possible flaw in my own, which might produce a disjointed paper of different styles from section to section. To remedy that possibility, read the entire manuscript through from beginning to end at one sitting. I hope it flows smoothly.

SUBMITTING THE MANUSCRIPT TO A JOURNAL

So far, I have written as though you knew the journal to which you would send your manuscript. Belatedly I advise you to consult APA's *Journals in Psychology: A Resource Listing for Authors* (4th ed.; 1993), not only to discover the publication most appropriate for your topic but also to learn its instructions for form and style. Then, study the APA *Manual* for details about type of paper, print, number of copies, and so on.

Before you put the manuscript in the mail, be sure that you have not already submitted it for review to some other journal and that its contents have not already been published elsewhere; to do otherwise is unethical. In the cover letter accompanying the manuscript, state that informed consent was obtained if you studied humans, and that you have complied with the relevant APA guidelines if you studied animals. Note also that you are duty-bound to keep the raw data not only throughout the review process but for another 5 years after the manuscript is accepted.

Prepare yourself to wait several weeks for a response from the editor, perhaps as long as 16 weeks—as long, that is, as the usual college semester. Time is required to choose the appropriate reviewers, for each reviewer to study the manuscript and to write the review, and for editors to weigh the reviews and compose their own reviews—concurring, disagreeing, reconciling—to reach the final decision. A humorous editorial in *Science* once lampooned an investigator impatient and irate over the delay in learning the fate of his submitted manuscript, while at the same time, as the reviewer of a manuscript, he was defending his own tardiness to a demanding editor.

If your manuscript is accepted with suggestions for only minor revisions, rejoice, for it is a rare event among APA journals (Eichorn & VandenBos, 1985). If it is rejected "with option to revise and resubmit"— the more common positive decision—take heart. Although even well-intentioned criticism is hard to take, this is no time for tender feelings. Accord each comment and suggestion the most serious attention; some just might be justified and, if attended to, would strengthen your presentation. Often you are asked for more detail about the method or told to shorten the manuscript, especially the discussion. Sometimes what is clear to you is not to another; I recall that when Helen Koch, my advisor, would challenge a sentence in a draft of my dissertation and I would tell her what it meant, she would respond, "But that's not what you wrote." Certainly, if you have followed my advice and studied the APA *Manual*, the criticism of "poorly written" will never be leveled against you.

When you return the revised manuscript, include a letter to the editor listing the changes made in response to the recommendations and explaining why you may be rejecting some. Editors and reviewers are earnest and hard-working but not infallible. Gently, oh so gently, guide them when they are uninformed and correct them when they are wrong. In the last paragraph, thank the editor and reviewers for their efforts; that their efforts are indeed helpful is apparent in the many journal articles in which authors thank "the anonymous reviewers."

On the other hand, now consider that your manuscript has been rejected—for that journal at that time. You can of course send it to another journal. Or, you might relive Underwood's (1957) reactions to his manuscript's rejection: "(a) one day of depression; (b) one day of utter contempt for the editor and his accomplices; (c) one day of decrying the conspiracy against letting Truth be published; (d) one day of fretful ideas about changing my profession; (e) one day of re-evaluating the manuscript in view of the editor's comments followed by the conclusion that I was lucky it wasn't accepted!" (p. 87). What he doesn't tell us, but what we can assume, is that on the sixth day he set to work.

As you finish reading this section, you well may ask, "What! All this work for just one publication?" The answer is "Yes!" Just about every research report you read was labored over this diligently, and some even more intensively as they were reworked, rewritten, and re-reviewed to satisfy an editor's requirements. So, meet the task head-on, prepared to give it its due, and may a sense of wry good humor sustain you in your labors.

11

OBTAINING A GRANT

The practice of applying for a grant to support empirical research has become so common today that it seems almost obligatory. Yet Harvey Carr (1936) in his autobiography expressed the opinion that many excellent experiments could be performed without what he called "that modern accessory device—the subsidy" (while admitting that his attitude was probably colored by his never having had one) (p. 80). I recall, also, that Edward Thorndike (1898) observed the associative processes of chicks in pens made of "books stuck up on end"—an ingenious device, admirably simple and efficient, but surely too casual and imprecise to meet the demands of today's granting agencies. Interestingly, because Harvard could not provide space for his studies, Thorndike studied the chicks in the cellar of William James's house.

These echoes of the past aside, today almost any research you plan costs money. If you study animals, you need money for their care. If you study humans, you need money to travel to them or to bring them to your laboratory. For both, you may need stimulating and recording equipment, often sophisticated and expensive. Salaries for assistants, graduate students, and even yourself (as during a summer) may be required. And always there are costs for clerical supplies and computer time—to conclude a bare and incomplete account for any particular study. When your own institution cannot supply these necessities, you must find some other source.

Although the only reason for seeking financial support is to conduct the research, obtaining it possesses other advantages. It qualifies as a mark of prestige for you (often considered as such in the awarding of tenure and promotion in academic settings) and for your department and institution, to which it also supplies valuable "overhead" funds. Furthermore, a grant can provide financial support for the training of the students who assist your efforts. Let me add, too, that whether you obtain the grant or not, the applying by itself is favorably viewed by your colleagues.

Complain as we do about the time and effort required to prepare a grant application, we could make the task less onerous for ourselves by casting it in a more positive light. First, it does provide the stimulus to define your question sharply and clearly, shorn of the usual fuzziness of ideas not yet put in writing. It also demands that you once again cover the literature and causes you to think twice about the hard facts of time and money, space and resources. In short, to prepare a grant proposal is to translate your dream into reality.

Before you apply, give some thought to the responsibility you incur if you are awarded a grant. True, you have not signed a contract to produce certain results (although there are contract-type awards), but you are obligated to pursue the research. In many cases you will be spending taxpayers' dollars, and, regardless of its source, money for research is always in short supply and to be spent thriftily. Furthermore, a grant also places a responsibility on your institution, because in point of fact the grant is awarded to it, and you are only the instrument of fulfilling the promise. Be prepared for a constant (I toyed with the adjective *relentless*) sense of pressure to discharge the obligation; while living with grants, I was ever conscious of justifying to myself even reading jaunts to the student bookstore. Then, as research is not following a recipe, you will need to remain alert to new leads to pursue, within the constraints of your general topic. And, not to draw too doleful a picture, time passes quickly, and soon you will have to prepare an annual report to qualify for continuing support.

FINDING A SOURCE OF SUPPORT

The first step in seeking support begins not with finding a source but with formulating your ideas about the research for which you need support (for a good statement, see the Supplement by William Redd in chapter 7). These ideas will have developed over a period of years from your interests, reading, and experience; they do not arise full-blown the moment you look for support. Guides, workshops, and tapes on how to find a source of support, and even on how to prepare an application, offer no help on that most important element of any proposal: the research you wish to conduct.

To be lured by money belies one's sense of purpose even as it violates the ethics of the scientific enterprise. Success in dollars alone would be an empty achievement, spelling just work without the joy of pursuing one's own deepest interests. My solicitude for your future as an earnest scholar and investigator is probably misplaced; from my experience as a reviewer of applications, I know how quickly my colleagues sense the tenuous relationship between proposals driven by the quest for money and the proposers' past interests and achievements.

If you are just beginning an independent research career, find out if your institution has any funds to support research. Small though such funds usually are, they offer many advantages. First, the simpler form of the application gives you practice in preparing the more complex document required by external agencies. Then, including the award in your CV attests to the successful outcome of at least one critical review. Most important, however, the funds enable you to get to work. The small amount of money has other advantages: It forces you to think small, to attack problems that offer a reasonable chance of being completed in a couple of years, and above all, it provides data for a research report. Thus do you begin to build a "track record."

As you carry out research, new ideas for future work come to mind, and a program of related studies begins to take form. Although no one has yet shown a positive relation between amounts of money spent and the significance of the results, there comes a time when you will need more money to realize that program. For such money, many federal, state, and private agencies are committed to supporting different areas of research. Academic officers and librarians can lead you to guides, catalogs, registers, and directories of these many sources, as well as to electronic bulletin boards, especially the APA's Research Psychology Funding Bulletin, available via BITNET or INTERNET. From them you can learn much to further your quest for an appropriate agency. Many agencies also publish annual reports of the research they support, the names of officers from whom you can obtain more information, and the names of the scientists who serve on their review panels. Then, on your own, you can identify the sources of support acknowledged in the journal articles that report studies close to your own topic of research.

Cast a wide net, study the wealth of information available, and consult your mentors and colleagues. Then telephone or write the program officer of your choice to learn if your plan, given in a few sentences, meets the agency's interests. If so, you will be sent an application.

PREPARING THE APPLICATION

Although the form of the application differs by agencies, all have in common these main parts: a statement of purpose, supporting background, method of study, significance of the research, facilities available, estimated costs, a CV, and approval of the research by an ethics committee. Whatever the order in which these parts are to be presented and whatever the degree of detail required, be sure to follow the application's guidelines exactly.

Start by composing the statement of purpose. It is the most important as well as the most difficult part, so write it first—so you can revise it again and again. On the basis of this statement, compose a strong and incisive title. Titles are not everything, but they are important; like a logo, a title identifies you and your idea. Then, present the main objectives simply, clearly, and concisely, and do not hesitate to make them sound as interesting and provocative as they in fact are to you.

Next, weigh each of the objectives in relation to what is already known. Then, in a few paragraphs of closely reasoned statements, show how that knowledge provides the basic premises from which you work and leads directly to your plan. Search the literature widely enough to include the earliest work, while not ignoring the more recent, and be sure to mention your own contributions. The choice of references should be discriminating and strictly limited to the statement of purpose and objectives. A mass of carelessly assembled references will cost you dearly.

Now present the design of how you intend to achieve the main objectives. Go into detail about the techniques of gathering and analyzing data. Who are the subjects and how are they selected? What variables are you manipulating and how will you measure their effect? What results do you expect, and why? You need to present only one or two studies in detail, and any others in outline. Just here you want to show that you know research is a foray into the unknown; to that end, explain that the results of early efforts may lead you to revise the plans for subsequent work.

At this juncture in the writing, you face a stringent test of the proposal: Can you accomplish the work in the few years for which you are asking support? Pause to consider that there are subjects to obtain, assistants to train, apparatus to design, supplies to order, procedures to establish (and perhaps to revise), data to analyze, and annual reports to write. Revise the plan now before reviewers fault it for promising more than can be achieved.

Just in case the importance of your ideas may not be self-evident to your readers, in the section asking for their significance, tell in vivid but honest language how the findings will contribute to knowledge or solve a pressing theoretical or social problem. Be guided here by the avowed interests of the agency; if the agency was carefully chosen, you should not need to work hard at tailoring your idea of the research's value to meet its interests. Flights of fancy or exaggerated claims will do you no good. Nevertheless, use your imagination and soar a bit—it is, after all, your dream—but temper the soaring with reality.

The rest of an application calls for such practical matters as your resources for conducting the research and what more you need. What does your setting provide in space, laboratories, apparatus, computers, and statistical and secretarial support? Needs for personnel, equipment, travel costs, supplies, and so on must be precisely enumerated and conscientiously justified. Do not pad the budget; padding shows and hurts you. As you work out the budget, consult the business office of your institution to obtain current estimates of costs, as well as instruction on how to calculate the indirect costs. Enlisting the help of this office early ensures its later approval of the final budget. To complete the application, there remain only a copy of your CV and a statement of approval from the local ethical review committee, dated and signed by the designated officer of your institution.

As with any manuscript you write, ask your mentors, colleagues, and students for comments and criticism. In the light of these, revise conscientiously. Polish the prose, paragraph by paragraph, sentence by sentence, word by word, to produce a letter-perfect document. I can understand how you might think that only your brilliant ideas count, but you would be surprised to know how widely reviewers believe that carelessness in the application foretells carelessness in the research. Then, if space permits, construct a table of contents with a generous number of headings that break long or complex passages, not only to key the reviewers to different parts but to ease their reading. Until you yourself are a reviewer of proposals, you cannot appreciate the value of an elegant format; it will not win approval for the contents, but it attests to the seriousness of your efforts and shows a concern for your readers, the reviewers.

Know that the reviewers of your proposal are knowledgeable persons, conversant with the literature and experienced in research. Not only have they themselves prepared many proposals, but they have reviewed many. They are alert to fuzzy statements and sensitive to bombast. Have the reviewers in mind as you prepare your application and give them something lively, innovative, and well designed.

THE APPLICATION UNDER REVIEW

Funding agencies seek the judgment of scientists recognized for their competence as scholars and investigators—the process of peer review. Sometimes the reviewers meet as a committee, and other times they serve as ad hoc reviewers who mail in their assessments. All review the applications for scientific merit, originality, and significance. They also weigh the adequacy of the experimental approach; the training, experience, and competence or promise of the investigator; the suitability of available facilities; the reasonableness of the budget; and the provisions for protecting human and nonhuman subjects from risk and discomfort. From experience I can attest to how seriously they take the responsibility.

You can obtain information on how different agencies review proposals from publications such as *APA's Guide to Research Support* (Herring, 1987). Whatever the agency's procedures, you should be prepared for the time that will elapse between your mailing the proposal and learning its fate. Weeks, and more likely months, may pass while the agency reviews it and reaches a decision. For example, it may take as many as 8 months for applications to be sent to the reviewers and then reviewed in committee meetings, for the opinions and ratings to be reviewed by the advisory councils, and for funding finally to be determined by the ratings (the priority scores) in relation to the availability of money. Therefore, do not start making breathless trips to the mailbox for quite a while.

If that trip brings word of an award, rejoice! If you are one of the many for whom it does not, read on.

TRYING AGAIN

From the beginning of applying for a grant, doubts assailed you—in fact, to apply for a grant is to know how uncertainty and hope can live together. Fortunately, hope sustained the effort. But now you have failed and it hurts. You are entitled to sympathy, but rise like the phoenix. Take a couple of days to grieve, then get back to work—and the sooner the better.

Study as dispassionately as you can why the agency rejected your proposal. If reasons were not given in its summary, you are entitled to request them from the program director or executive officer. If the proposal was deemed not appropriate for the interests of the agency, you can of course submit it to another, more appropriate agency; that's a simple solution. Otherwise, you should consider the criticisms, revise the application as you see fit, and resubmit it. Was the purpose of the proposal not clear, the method lacking in detail, the review of the literature incomplete, the design inadequate to achieve the main objectives, or were the time and money budgets unrealistic? Turn to your mentors and colleagues for advice. Be sure to include in the revision the results of any relevant work you accomplished in the months while you were awaiting an answer. Or even now take time to apply once again to a local funding source for a small grant to answer some specific shortcoming. Then, when you do send the revision, call attention to the changed parts in the application by indenting, bracketing, underlining, or changing the type of the appropriate passage— and, to leave nothing to chance, accompany the revision with a letter enumerating the significant changes.

A salutary view of seeking grant support can be entertained despite its frequent disappointments. First, if you have a sound idea for which you need financial support, there is indeed a considerable amount of money available. True, the competition for it is keen. Yet just as you seek support, agencies also seek worthy projects to support. Besides, no matter what the outcome, your time and energy are not wasted in preparing an application. To apply provides the stimulus to organize your thoughts and to cast the plan in terms of time, services, and money, thus preventing a headstrong and undisciplined attack. Inasmuch as you ought as a matter of course to write a detailed plan before beginning the research, a grant application can be seen as only a more formal and polished statement thereof. Moreover, by submitting the proposal to the scrutiny of experts, you obtain invaluable advice. The saddest mistake you can make is not to apply; the next saddest is not to apply again.

Up to this point I have discussed only applications for grant support originated independently by an individual investigator and limited still further to empirical research. Guides supply information on many other possibilities, such as requests for research on specific topics; program projects; research career development awards; and special awards for women, minorities, persons with disabilities, and new and young investigators. Despite their variety, all share the same basic elements presented in this section. Once you master them, you have acquired the skills to apply for different awards.

To be sure, study the guides, attend workshops that promise help in getting your proposal to the right place and the right person at the right time, or tap into computer bulletin boards, day or night, for current information on programs. But there is no magic word. There is no "open sesame." Once you have a sparkling idea for which you need money, what works is work.

IV

THE YEARS OF INFLUENCE

12

SERVING YOUR INSTITUTION

As professors, our influence extends far beyond the classroom, even beyond the effect we have on our students, for with but a few years' experience, we begin to carry responsibilities for our institution, our discipline, and our professional associations, and for the social and civic agencies of our society. By portraying them here, I throw them into relief so you can recognize, and appreciate, how they affect events outside the classroom.

These responsibilities lie ready at hand, ours to assume or not, given the freedom we cherish. Some professors regard these activities as unwelcome intrusions in a life of scholarship; others see them as obligations, reasonable and fitting for their membership in academe. They are, of course, opportunities to widen your horizon and develop new skills—even as they enrich your work in the classroom and laboratory.

On campuses everywhere, the professor's activities are spelled out as teaching, scholarship, research, and service. We have a fairly good understanding of what is meant by teaching, scholarship, and research, but what exactly does service mean? Surely, we serve our students by teaching and the world at large by advancing knowledge, but service would seem to encompass more: precisely what I have been saying about those activities beyond our desks—that is, serving our institution, our discipline, and the public interest. But now, having separated service into categories, I see how tenuous is the division, for, in fact, they are almost indivisible.

To illustrate how entwined the categories are, I consider my service in 1966 as a consultant to a project sponsored by the Pan American Health Organization's Institute of Nutrition of Central America and Panama (IN-CAP). Our team traveled to Guatemala to plan how to measure the effect of improved nutrition on the physical and mental development of Guatemalan children. As I think about the assignment now, I see how many different classes of service it fulfilled: It provided a measure of recognition for my university (the chancellor could include my service in the annual report) and for my discipline as a source of information about not only experimental design but also tests and measurements; it tried to solve a pressing human need; and at the same time, it enriched my teaching by giving me a real-life problem to share with my students.

Thus, for many activities that a professor engages in, such as refereeing a journal article, serving on a search committee for a new provost, or planning a children's museum, the nature of the service is varied and the agencies served are many. Do not be misled about the relative importance of the different areas of service by my unequal treatment of them; the greater attention I accord to participating in the affairs of one's discipline reflects only my own experiences rather than a conviction about the lesser importance of serving the public or one's school. For any one person—for you—one or another activity will assume greater importance, perhaps different activities at different times in your life, and always specific to the mission of your institution.

As professors, we tend to think that we and the students *are* the school, and indeed I have often seen the faculty referred to as the school's "heart and mind." We not only speak of governing ourselves but jealously guard the right to do so. In fact, however, we only share in the governing (even if in some areas we do have near-complete authority), because the final authority in institutions of higher learning resides in their governing boards, although they delegate some of that power to the president (or chancellor), who in turn recognizes the areas over which the provost, deans, and faculty have primary responsibility. These matters are discussed by Pye (1988) and are set forth in the Joint Statement on Government of Colleges and Universities of the AAUP (1990a).

Parenthetically speaking, I continue to be impressed with the power the AAUP exerts in enunciating and protecting the authority that faculty members possess. Since 1915 it has been a strong friend of the faculty, its principles endorsed by scores of professional and educational institutions and woven into the bylaws of many colleges and universities. This self-appointed arbiter of correct practices maintains a chapter on every campus and would welcome you as a member.

What part do you, as a professor, actually play in the governing of your institution? At first, the question won't interest you, but it will more and more as you see what you think should be improved. I begin with the courses you teach, and remind you once again that, within the stated mission of your institution, you are the sole arbiter of what you teach, how you teach, and what constitutes a student's mastery. Now, however, your courses must fit with those of the other professors in the department to form a major course of study. Thus, in department meetings, you and your colleagues—as your field develops—will add courses, revise some, and drop others, continually working to construct a coherent course of study.

Beyond the courses your department offers, your authority also extends to the curriculum required for degrees, both undergraduate and graduate. Your voice is sought and heard in the faculty's deliberations on the curriculum as a whole—the number of course hours required for graduation, the distribution of courses among the different areas of study, and the importance of writing and speaking. These are decisions that professors are called upon to make again and again as they define and redefine the characteristics of the educated person. And within that curriculum, you will often be called upon to participate in recommending to the dean and the provost new areas of study, as fields of knowledge expand, divide, and coalesce.

Your authority as a faculty member also extends to aspects of the students' lives that affect their intellectual development. For example, fresh in my mind is the recent work of a faculty committee on my campus to establish academic criteria for admitting athletes to the university and for monitoring their scholastic progress. Going further, it not only reduced the number of trips for games away from the campus but limited the length of the athletic season.

The second major area of your "authority" as a professor encompasses responsibility for the academic quality of your department. You and your fellow professors will advise the chair on who will join you—that is, on who will be appointed, reappointed, promoted, and granted tenure. Whereas not so many years ago these decisions were made about you, now you are making them about others. You are thinking about the candidate's competence and collegiality in relation to the needs of your students and the department, and about the effect of the decision on the reputation of the department, which in turn affects not only your institution's reputation but your own.

You have still other opportunities to influence events. Professors are regularly consulted about the appointment of the chair or head of their department and, often, as members of search committees, about the appointments of deans, provosts, directors of institutes, and even of chancellors and presidents. Furthermore, faculty members set their own rules for conducting business in their councils or senates and form a host of committees to consider such matters as faculty welfare and grievances, the status of women and minority persons, and the granting of honorary degrees.

As professors we guard these responsibilities zealously. We believe that we have the competence to judge such matters, that we can be counted on to be just and generous, and that without a doubt we have the good of the students, the department, and the institution at heart. (See this chapter's Supplement, "Integrity as a Faculty Member" by Lyle V. Jones.) All in all, then, although you do not run your school, you do have considerable influence and virtually complete responsibility with respect to the courses of study, the character of your department, the choice of colleagues, and all matters pertaining to the students' academic life. The faculty is, in my admittedly biased view, first among equals.

SUPPLEMENT

INTEGRITY AS A FACULTY MEMBER

LYLE V. JONES

University of North Carolina at Chapel Hill

May 1993

A prospective faculty member harbors a number of career goals relating to teaching, scholarship, and professional service. Aspiring to be an outstanding teacher is admirable; yet some successful and influential faculty members display classroom teaching that, while adequate, is not exceptionally effective. An intention to excel in research and scholarly publication is highly appropriate; however, a few academic psychologists who have failed to develop a coherent program of research or publication are nonetheless stimulating colleagues, highly regarded and widely respected. The wish to provide good service to one's department, college or university, and community is laudable, but failing to excel in such activity does not automatically disqualify a faculty member from career satisfaction or eminence. The one *essential* ingredient for success as a faculty member is consistent personal integrity, based on the maintenance of high standards in all aspects of academic life.

A student's beliefs as to what distinguishes effective from less effective faculty members develop from observing many instructors over the course of undergraduate and graduate study. Seldom is one or more of those instructors consciously chosen as a "model," and yet their influences can be powerful; for students who later become faculty members, those influences establish the predisposition to behave in certain ways. Students are most fortunate if the greatest influence has been exercised by professionally successful and personally honorable faculty mentors. Often that is the case, because students recognize, admire, and tend to emulate faculty members who are dedicated to their work, who have challenged them to exert maximal performance, who are perceived to have treated all students fairly and with respect, and who are recognized for their personal integrity.

The initial years of your first faculty appointment are exhilarating and challenging. You map out the institutional terrain, develop a research agenda, establish or strengthen ties with others in your specialty area, build new relations with departmental colleagues, prepare classroom activities, and react to the stimulation of students, all the while meeting a raft of unfamiliar new responsibilities. Values and habits formed in this initial faculty term remain indelibly inscribed for the remainder of your career; the great importance of careful good judgment in establishing those values and habits may not be fully recognized. Career-long criteria should prevail, even if they conflict with tempting short-term rewards. Maintaining and enhancing personal integrity is the key not only to a rewarding career, but also to reinforcing the kind of departmental and institutional integrity that is so essential for maintaining quality in education.

INTEGRITY IN TEACHING

Not everyone becomes an inspirational teacher, no matter how great an effort is exerted. However, every faculty member can and should strive to find ways to involve students in learning and to employ fair and consistent standards in the evaluation of students. Thorough preparation for classes is essential, as is showing concern for students. Grades must be influenced by the relevant performance of students, and by nothing else. Whether a student is male or female, Black, Hispanic, Asian, White, or "other," handicapped or not, personally liked or disliked by the professor—all of these are impermissible grounds for grading. Equal treatment and encouragement should be provided to all students. (For only the most saintly among us is that effort likely to succeed totally, but striving for such perfection remains a worthy and useful goal.)

With respect to integrity, faculty members do serve as models. One instrument of direct influence on the behavior of students is a consistently strict policy with regard to cheating. Every instructor should take pains to explain that cheating will not be tolerated, and then should responsibly implement that policy by scrupulously following institutional procedures whenever anyone has engaged in cheating. Some instructors find this course to be distasteful; it can be not only time-consuming, but also emotionally demanding. To fail in this regard, however, is unfair to all of your students, untrue to the policies of the institution, and—most importantly—untrue to yourself.

Teaching at every level should entail not only classroom activity, but also individual tutelage and research sponsorship. Individual attention is especially prevalent at the graduate level, where it is highly desirable that you be perceived as even-handed. Faculty members sometimes are viewed by graduate students as having favorites (those who participate in an instructor's research program, for example) and of making lesser demands on those favored students than on others. The flip side of this is also quite unfortunate: the belief that a faculty member holds grudges against some students, for whom academic progress thus is made more difficult. In a department with a few such faculty members, politicization is likely to ensue, student and faculty cliques are formed, and the freedom to express views openly is jeopardized—all of which is detrimental to a healthy environment for learning and scholarship.

A pitfall sometimes not recognized until too late is that of forming close personal friendships with selected undergraduate or graduate students. If these have amorous or sexual overtones, results can be devastating. But even in the absence of romance, other students may suspect that the student friend is receiving favorable treatment beyond that earned by academic performance. Whether or not the suspicions are warranted, tensions arise that are awkward for the concerned parties, and that may lead to charges of favoritism, unprofessional conduct, or, in some cases, sexual harassment. You must recognize and respect the fine line between the constructive development of supportive relations with students on the one hand and the establishment of illicit alliances with selected students on the other.

INTEGRITY IN RESEARCH AND PUBLICATION

Honesty and integrity in conducting research and in reporting on the research design, execution, and findings are an absolute imperative. Not only must all relevant features of a research effort be described fully in research publications, but care should be taken to document such features as a project progresses, and documentation and data should be retained (available for sharing with others) for at least a decade following publication. Science is a self-correcting process. Researchers must support that process with a willing commitment to share their data with others as soon as their analyses have been released for publication.

Questions often arise as to who are the appropriate authors of a research publication. Students or colleagues who contribute significantly to a research project should be invited to be coauthors. It must be understood that coauthorship entails the willingness to fully share responsibility for all phases of research and for the entire content of research reports. Each author must sign off on the draft and approve all subsequent changes in the text. Order of authorship should be discussed and agreed upon early in the research process, to minimize misunderstandings and acrimony that become more likely when that decision is delayed. The listed order either may be alphabetically determined or may reflect an order of responsibility and effort; it may be appropriate to add a footnote in the published report to indicate which principle was invoked.

In recent years, the numbers of charges of research misconduct and of fraudulent research have markedly increased. Essentially all universities and other research institutions now have developed policies by which such charges, if promulgated, will be investigated. It is wise to become familiar with your institutional guidelines for ethical research practices and for the investigation of complaints, to assure that you never violate the conditions of fair practice and that you are aware of the consequences of any charge of misconduct.

A recurrent feature of research articles found to have been fraudulent is that of multiple authorship, often involving authors at different institutions, some of whom had little or no role in the research being reported. Although there are other sound reasons for not accepting invitations to become an "honorary" author of a research report, the avoidance of career-threatening association with possibly fraudulent research certainly must be viewed as a compelling one.

A somewhat different set of guidelines apply to responsibilities for administering research funds. Sponsored research grants and contracts provide monies that may not be spent for purposes unrelated to the approved research activities. The fundamental responsibility for assuring the proper use of research funding resides with the principal investigator (PI) or project director. It cannot be delegated; if it is nominally delegated, the PI nevertheless remains the effective locus of responsibility. The PI not only must be vigilant to assure the appropriate use of funds by research personnel, but also must guard against the possible diversion of research funds by superiors—laboratory directors, department chairs, institutional research administrators, purchasing departments, and so on. Except for overhead receipts, a budget for sponsored research is made up of direct expenses that are associated with that research; the use of those funds for other purposes is both illegal and immoral, and the PI must be able to guarantee that no funds will be expended inappropriately.

Special challenges to integrity have been created by the "time and effort" reports for research personnel that are required for most federal research grants and contracts. In an effort to simplify reporting while still meeting federal requirements, our institutions have developed forms to be approved periodically by the PI, listing a percentage of effort, for each person paid from each research grant, equal to the percentage of salary paid to that person from the grant. At some institutions, percentages are listed to three places—for example, 38.5%. Can you honestly attest that exactly 38.5% of your effort, or that of a research colleague, was devoted to a particular research project last month? You are required either to do so, or to change the percentage to another specific figure (thus inviting serious repercussions from accounting and payroll offices). At institutions where faculty members or others are paid for 9 months' service in 12 monthly installments, the complexities of this reporting system are greatly exacerbated. How can a PI honestly manage this requirement? Each PI must let conscience guide behavior. The basic problem is that a bureaucratic set of procedures has been adopted that, if followed, inevitably makes of every PI a perjurer. Our institutions tell us that the procedures must be followed. Our consciences tell us that these procedures should be reconsidered and changed.

INTEGRITY IN SERVICE

You might think that the greatest challenges to a faculty member's integrity would arise in the context of teaching or research. The importance of those challenges should not be minimized but, arguably, more frequent temptations occur in the exercise of academic citizenship: as a participant in faculty meetings and in faculty committee deliberations, discussing degree requirements, curricula, space allocations, faculty appointments, promotions, or tenure matters. Often, in such deliberations, you must set aside your own short-sighted interests in favor of long-range benefits to the department or the institution. All too frequently, however, faculty members are able to delude themselves by rationalizing that selfish views also best serve institutional values. Alas, that can erode your integrity; over time, it erodes also your power to influence decision making.

The importance of adhering to principles of objectivity and to long-range criteria for decision making is magnified when you serve on university-wide committees. Here, you should distance yourself from narrow departmental interests in order best to serve the needs of the institution as a whole.

It goes without saying that, in service to the community outside your college or university, your responsibilities to the institution should not be forgotten. Great damage can be done to the institution—and ultimately to one's own career—if misunderstandings or disagreements within the academy are carried outside with the intention of building political pressures for one position or another. Even when issues of fundamental principle are involved, all avenues of appeal within the institution should be exhausted prior to considering an appeal for outside help. Even then, you should take a broad perspective, trying to understand the possibly principled positions of your opponents, before deciding whether to compromise or stand firm. Such a perspective may require a "cooling-off period," especially for cases in which it is difficult to separate personal animosities from logical arguments.

As in all walks of life, faculty members may find themselves unexpectedly facing dilemmas if matters of deep personal principle are in conflict with employment requirements. In such cases, hard choices must be made: submitting to the requirements, resigning from employment, or seeking legal redress (probably at considerable cost). A classic example at many public universities, some decades ago, resulted from state laws requiring that, as a condition of employment, all teaching personnel sign an oath disclaiming affiliation with any of a large number of political organizations (decreed to have been "Communist-front" societies). Although most faculty members found this requirement to be repugnant, most also signed. Some refused, and were unemployed, often pending court decisions—sometimes favorable, but occasionally not supporting the plaintiff's position. When choices of that kind are forced upon faculty members, there is an erosion of morale and a general threat to both personal and institutional integrity. Through individual soul searching and thoughtful consideration, you must hope to make that personal decision that best reduces the net damage to your career goals on the one hand and your personal integrity on the other.

13

SERVING YOUR DISCIPLINE

In everything we do as professors, we serve our discipline, but for want of a heading under which to include activities beyond teaching and research, I use the title "Serving Your Discipline." Herein I consider our activities as members of professional societies, as writers of scholarly works and organizers of knowledge, and as judges of what best furthers psychology as a science and a profession.

PARTICIPATING IN PROFESSIONAL SOCIETIES

The purposes, standards, and activities of our professional and learned societies are set and carried out by their members—that is, by you and me. We elect members to serve as officers, and we serve, if elected. Among a host of other concerns, as members of boards and committees, we set requirements for membership and fellow status, for the accrediting of academic programs, and for ethical conduct. Unlike our status as professors in colleges and universities, in our professional associations we share responsibility with no higher academic authority; having full authority, we share it only with each other.

At the annual conventions of these societies, we tell each other what we are thinking about and what we have found out. Unlike putting one's work into print, presenting it at a convention brings an audience's immediate response.

Fortunately, societies issue the call for contributions to the program months in advance of the meeting, thus giving you time to decide which category of presentation (posters, symposia, talks, etc.) best fits your ideas. Posters, the preferred mode of presenting research data, provide a wonderful exercise to help you find the most important ideas within your seemingly complex study. Indeed, to design a poster presents a challenge: how to convert the many pages of the study's purpose, method, results, and significance into just a few sheets of paper—and even half of these few will be graphic displays of your "take home" message.

If you are invited to participate in a symposium, do not stray from the symposium's theme to matters of your own interest, as many impolitely do, and do refer often to the findings and opinions of the other members of the symposium. If you are invited to be the discussant, be generous in your appraisal of the papers; emphasize their strengths and tread softly on any weaknesses, so that the members will be pleased to have so perceptive a reader of their efforts.

Even more demanding is the role of a chairperson. You open the symposium by tracing the theme's background and its place in current inquiries. To honor the speakers, add a few biographical details as you introduce them, and a brief sketch of their achievements. On you falls the onerous task of holding the speakers to their allotted time and of saving a goodly amount of time for a discussion between the participants and the audience. Finally, conclude the session with a lively and spirited summary. Given these many tasks, you had best compose your introduction and conclusion in the quiet of your study so that you can rise above the untoward distractions all too frequent at conventions. As you prepare for this demanding role, keep in mind Sindermann's (1982) words: "Next to superb presentations of papers, there is little that contributes more to the success of a session than an outstanding performance by the person chairing it" (p. 76).

Consider now that you wish to organize a symposium at the convention; you see how your work and interests mesh with those of others to raise a timely question. As the theme takes shape, assemble a list of possible candidates, and invite the likely ones at once. Give them the theme, your reason for including them, and the names of the others you intend to invite. If your proposal is accepted, complete the paperwork on schedule. Then, at the convention, perhaps the night before the symposium, try to arrange an informal get-together of the members so they will meet on the platform as friends with a common purpose. On the day of the symposium, survey the meeting room early on to test the microphones and visual aids equipment. Although much of the success of a symposium depends on the chairperson, as I have said, even more depends on you, the organizer. Did you conceive a lively, interesting, and important theme? How astute was your choice of participants?

In conclusion, do look with favor on presenting your work and ideas at your society's convention. It is a pleasant and rewarding way to honor your duty as a scholar and a scientist to offer your work to an open forum. The feedback is prompt (and therefore all the more valuable), and you become known as more than a name on a piece of paper. Furthermore, when you take part in the program, you begin to feel responsible for the scientific, as well as the professional, values of your society. Something else happens—an emotional experience that I can capture by these few words: To participate is to know first a stretch of uncertainty, then a flush of anticipation, and finally the glow of accomplishment.

ACCEPTING INVITATIONS

As your work becomes known, you may be invited to share your findings and thoughts with others beyond your institution—for example, to give a colloquium, to write a chapter for a book, or to participate in a conference, the proceedings of which may be published.

Presenting a Colloquium

If you think you have something of interest to say, accept the invitation. We learn not only by setting our thoughts down on paper but also by hearing ourselves say them, especially to a fresh audience. Then, if you plan your presentation properly, you will get comments and questions that cause you to amend, revise, strengthen, and even extend your own thoughts. By planning properly, I mean ending early enough to allow time for questions, as well as the more difficult maneuver of here and there slipping in a dogmatic or controversial statement to evoke a challenge.

On the matter of financial compensation, beyond travel expenses, an honorarium is welcome, but I would not make it a condition of acceptance. No monetary value can be placed on your contribution, especially when you are also often asked to meet students, to conduct a class, or to speak words of wisdom at social gatherings. Nor can the usual honorarium compensate you for the effort the visit costs in arranging for your absence from office, classes, and home and in handling the work that awaits you on your return. George Albee (1984) has written humorously of how much is often asked of a colloquium speaker and how arrangements of dates and travel can go astray. The trials of the famous notwithstanding, I take a more favorable view of such an invitation. You were selected (sometimes by both students and faculty) from a host of other possibilities, and you will be treated as someone special—a welcome contrast with your everyday life at home. Indeed, for most persons, giving a colloquium is a heartening experience.

Writing a Chapter

Here a respected person in your field invites you to write a chapter for a book designed to treat a single well-defined theme—not just a review of your already published work, but a fresh and original statement of new findings, hypotheses, and thoughts related to the theme of the book. Unlike the formal structure of a journal article, a chapter lets you present interesting details and expound your beliefs and opinions. In the process you may well arrive at some new insights and a firmer conception of the course of your future work. (I skip over the matter of royalties because the amount of money is negligible.)

These advantages notwithstanding, take time to weigh the invitation. Is your work ready for so comprehensive a treatment? Would a coauthor be helpful? Can you meet the deadlines? Will the preparation distract you from other assignments and duties? Given the interests and achievements of the editor and the other authors, is this book the proper place for your contribution? Then, can the editor be counted on to bring the book to press in a reasonable amount of time? Many a chapter has been written but never published in the planned volume because an author or two failed to meet the deadline. As you turn the invitation over in your mind, consider that, even though the editor may call for revisions, your chapter is assured of publication. In some institutions, however, committees judging evidence for promotion look less favorably on a record that contains more chapters in books than scholarly papers and research reports in refereed journals.

Participating in a Conference

You may be invited by a person of some authority to present your work and ideas at a conference on an issue of interest and emerging importance. Conferences meet, often in some congenial setting, for 3 or 4 days, during which the participants informally present their work and thoughts. The close attention to each other's presentations and the often spirited discussions among respected and admired colleagues make for a heady experience. For example, I recall with great pleasure being a member in 1959 of the Tavistock Conference on Mother–Infant Interaction, convened by John Bowlby and held at the Ciba Foundation House in London (and then again in 1961, 1963, and 1965). Amid an influx of new ideas, I came to define my own theoretical position. New friendships were forged; I mention only Mary Ainsworth, John Bowlby, David Hamburg, Harry Harlow, Robert Hinde, and Rudolph Schaffer. Its venue—in London—was not a drawback! Last, but not least, the discussions spurred me to carry out studies that were reported in each of the four volumes of *Determinants of Infant Behaviour* (Rheingold, 1961, 1963, 1969; Rheingold & Keene, 1965). By myself, in the quiet of my study, I *might* have done as much—but in the absence of contrary evidence, I believe I owe a great deal to the conferences.

In conclusion, then, if the conference treats a topic to which you can contribute and includes participants whom you respect, count on a rewarding experience.

INITIATING SCHOLARLY ACTIVITIES

When you realize that your own work and interests relate to a larger question, one that is also receiving attention by others from somewhat different perspectives, the time has come to move that bright idea to center stage. Now I reverse your previous roles, from contributor to a book to its editor, and from member of a conference to its organizer. Both new roles are valued by your colleagues, but neither is to be undertaken lightly because each requires exquisite judgment in choosing participants, unflagging attention to their efforts, endless correspondence, and, if a book is planned, stringent editing. Worse yet, if you are less than inspired about the importance of your idea and less than diligent in its realization, you run the risk of the poor reviews accorded many multi-author books. (Not all conferences result in books, but as many do, I write to include them.)

Take time to develop a plan. Discuss it informally with colleagues and some respected authorities in the field. Devote some days to reviewing the literature to identify potential contributors. Could a coeditor extend your vision and share the work? Draw up a tentative list of alert, interested, and knowledgeable participants whom you know to be conscientious, so that, in Maeve O'Connor's (1979) words, "dilatory contributors do not undo the good work of the punctual ones" (p. 9). If you are planning a conference, choose a congenial site, and investigate sources of financial support to provide living costs and perhaps transportation for the participants. Then, finally, it is time to think about the form of publication: An edited volume needs a publisher and a contract, but the proceedings of a conference may instead be published as a journal supplement or monograph. Once all these matters have been settled, you are ready to approach the contributors.

Your letter of invitation will tell them what you yourself wanted to know when you were asked to contribute a chapter or join a conference: the theme, its significance and timeliness, the special part each participant would play in its development, and the other persons you are inviting. For a conference, time and place come next, and for writing a chapter, approximate length and deadlines. End with the plans for publication, the press or journal with which arrangements have been made, the proposed date of publication, and monetary rewards, if any. Then, don't let your invitations languish too long without a reply. Write again soon.

My peremptory words aside, your tone, of course, will be complimentary and even enticing. Active and productive scholars need generous lead times—as much as 6 to 8 months to attend a conference or write a paper, and another 4 months for a revision, with a somewhat different timetable if one or two meetings intervene. Then, with the time required for producing a book or monograph, it may take 18 to 24 months from the letter of invitation to the date of publication—that is, if all goes well.

From my own experience, I offer some additional advice. Plan a smaller, rather than a larger, conference to allow ample time for discussion. You, as the editor, are responsible for producing more than just a collection of chapters. Introductory and concluding chapters help to unify a book, as do statements at the beginning of sections that relate the chapters to each other and to the theme of the book. Plan on a continuing correspondence with the authors to inform them of the book's progress, to keep them on schedule, and to jog their possibly flagging interest. One final task, as demanding as any other, requires editing everyone's contribution to produce a readable book. Be brave here and suggest what should be cut, added, and revised, even in the prose of persons you stand in awe of. I once reorganized a chapter by T. C. Schneirla and even revised Harry Harlow's prose.

So far I have been writing about organizing a conference and editing its proceedings, but many other activities also qualify as scholarly contributions: writing a critical review of a challenging question, assembling a book of scholarly papers on a common theme and, above all, writing textbooks. (See "Writing a Textbook" [Supplement] by Ross Vasta, which follows.)

SUPPLEMENT

WRITING A TEXTBOOK

ROSS VASTA

State University of New York at Brockport

March 1992

One day it may happen. A colleague, a student, or even your spouse (if he or she is crazy) will suggest that you write a textbook. Or maybe the idea will be planted by a publisher's sales rep making a routine call at your office. Whatever the source, your thoughts will probably immediately race to several highly successful books that you know have brought their authors prestige, wealth, and a secure place in the annals of the discipline. Why not, then, you? Wouldn't this be a great way to gain recognition and respect in your field, to learn an enormous amount about your area and, of course, to make a bundle of money?

If the lure of writing a textbook has brought you to the point of seriously considering the possibility, it is important to get the whole story. Colleagues and sales reps may be well intentioned, but, in the final analysis, it is you who will be doing the work. This section examines some of the issues involved in preparing a major textbook in psychology. Although some of it is relevant also to the writing of smaller, paperback volumes on circum-scribed topics, the focus is on large-market texts for standard undergraduate courses.

CONDUCTING A REALITY CHECK

Although most prospective authors are naturally a bit starry-eyed, being out of touch with reality is a prescription for disappointment. Before doing anything, then, you need to come to grips with a few basic truths.

159

Writing a textbook requires an enormous amount of time and energy. Disabuse yourself of any notion that you will "do it on the side." If your book is going to be up-to-date—a feature that is important for most books and critical for some—you will need to complete it in a relatively short period of time (typically, 2–4 years). This won't happen if you work on it only on Saturday mornings. Besides, writing a book in small, spaced-out pieces may drag the project out interminably, given the need for repeated start-up and revision time. So plan to have the project become a prominent part of your professional and personal life.

You are not likely to get rich.. The competition among textbooks and publishers is very tough. Even if your book is reasonably successful, the amount of money you make—when measured against the many months of effort you have put into it—will hardly feel like a windfall. (One of my colleagues tells me he calculated his earnings to be about 70 cents an hour on his first edition.) Substantial monetary reward is usually realized only if the book goes on to a second or third edition, where the ratio of time investment to financial gain is much lower. But since many textbooks, even when written by well-known scholars and published by first-rate houses, do not survive beyond the first edition, you must be prepared for the possibility that the payback for all your effort will end after 3–4 years.

Textbooks rarely catapult authors to fame or spur rapid career advancement. The academic world displays a good deal of ambivalence toward textbook writing. In fact, at better schools, the writing of a survey text may not even be viewed as scholarship but rather as an enterprise that is largely nonintellectual and commercially driven. Another successful author-colleague once estimated it to be worth "about a minus two." Note, however, that this is less true at lower-level colleges and universities and also at institutions that view this kind of work as a pedagogical contribution to the discipline.

The previous caveat raises the more general question of whether this is the right point in your career to write a book. The time spent on the project will undoubtedly subtract from time you would otherwise have devoted to other scholarly activities. It is important to be sure that you are in a position to make this sacrifice. Textbook writing by untenured faculty members may be viewed warily by senior members of your department, and it would probably be wise to first float the idea past a few of them and maybe even your dean.

Your professional age may play a role also in the perspective you can bring to your writing. Most of us come out of graduate school somewhat narrower and more dogmatic than we will be 10 years later. Having a broader, more tolerant view of the field can often be a plus when preparing a textbook designed to appeal to a reasonably wide audience.

In short, writing a textbook is a long, tough road. It is crucial, therefore, that you have your eyes wide open before starting down it.

THE PLANNING STAGE

If the realities of the task have not completely discouraged you, there is still one major preliminary question: Is your basic idea viable?

For a textbook to be successful, it must get adopted. Writing a book that your colleagues read, admire, and cite, *but that they are not willing to use in their courses*, may stroke your ego, but it won't get you to a second edition. In publishing terms, you need to write a book that is marketable.

Satisfying this criterion requires doing some homework regarding the market. Perhaps the best source of market information is the competition. Get hold of the current textbooks from the leading publishers and try to determine how your market divides itself. Undoubtedly, one division will involve level: there will be long, rigorous books for Ivy League schools and briefer, lower-level books for state and community colleges. Some markets also are partitioned by text organization—for example, personality books are organized by theories or by research areas, clinical books are organized by therapy techniques or by problem areas, developmental books are chronological or topical. Less frequently, the market may be divided along theoretical lines, such as abnormal psychology books that are behavioral, humanistic, psychodynamic, or whatever.

First, decide where you want your book to fit into the existing scheme. The level is crucial: Too high, and it will be used only by professors to write their lectures; too low, and your colleagues (even at community colleges) will complain that you have overlooked significant information or have diluted important issues. On the other hand, it is the rare book that can appeal to the entire spectrum. So, realistically, your choice is between writing a book that is mid-to-upper level or one that is mid-to-lower level. Many authors make this decision based on the level of their own institution; it is easiest to write a book at the same level and scope as you are teaching. Decisions regarding organization, theoretical orientation, and the like are more dependent on personal preferences, but you should certainly take into account where you believe the field is going.

At this point you face what may be the most formidable challenge of the entire process. Textbook adoptions are strongly governed by the principle of inertia. Having set up a course and a series of lectures around a given textbook, the typical instructor will generally need a compelling reason to abandon that book. Your job is to provide that reason.

Publishers will tell you that an ideal new book should be about 70% conventional and 30% innovative. If you expect instructors to turn their course organizations upside-down or to cover vast amounts of new information, it's probably not going to happen. But you do need to get them excited (or at least intrigued) by what you have to offer that is new and different. This clearly is a tricky business, and precisely how you accomplish it will vary with your content area. In general, though, lower-level markets often are searching for more effective pedagogical techniques, whereas upper-level ones are likely to be wooed by a new thematic approach or the inclusion of a chapter on some hot new area of research.

FINDING A PUBLISHER

A crucial step in the book-writing process involves securing a contract with a publisher. It is generally best to do this early on in the project rather than after much of it is completed, for several reasons.

First, publishers will not invest in a project unless they are convinced it has a market and a reasonable chance of success. And since they know much more about these things than you do, it pays to heed their advice on this score (in fact, you may have no choice).

Second, the publisher can make your job easier by providing support—such as grant money to cover expenses, outside reviews of early chapters to provide feedback, and detailed information on which of your competitors is doing well and why.

For some authors, a third benefit of being under contract is motivational. The publisher will have a vested interest in keeping the project moving along, and this can't hurt on days when you would rather be working on your latest research idea or spending time on the golf course.

Assuming, then, that you have educated yourself as to the existing market and developed a plan for your entry into it, the next step is to put together a package of materials to submit to publishers. Usually a first-time author will be expected to supply one or two completed chapters to illustrate writing style, level of difficulty, pedagogical features, internal chapter organization, and so on. You should also outline the remainder of the book in as much detail as possible. Then, prepare a prospectus that includes such information as a description of the intended market (types of schools and specific courses in which it would be used), the major competing texts, distinctive characteristics of your organization or content, and pedagogical features. Submit this material under a cover letter that alludes to the 70–30% split discussed earlier. Publishers will be especially interested in your book's distinctive features, with an eye toward how a promotional campaign might be built around them.

The package should be sent to the psychology acquisitions editor, whose name you can get from your local sales rep. Sometimes the rep will offer to deliver the material and make the initial inquiries (note that reps get credit for discovering books that eventually get signed). This approach, however, places more responsibility in the hands of the rep than you may feel comfortable with, and the direct route is probably preferable.

Seeking a publisher is not the same as submitting a manuscript to a journal. You needn't hesitate to send it simultaneously to a number of publishing houses. If you get serious inquiries from more than one, all the better. Then you can compare what they have to offer.

If a publisher *is* interested in your plan, you will likely be contacted by the editor to whom you sent the materials. By this point, your package will probably have been sent out to several reviewers, so continued interest by the publisher suggests that they are ready to offer you a contract.

Negotiating your contract should be approached very seriously. Publishers may tell you that they have a "standard" contract for all their authors, but you, of course, know better. The details of what should go into a contract are too lengthy to be covered here. Consider, however, some of the kinds of questions that you should plan to raise: Will your book be black-and-white, or will it include some color (which is much more expensive)? Who will pay for the permissions to reprint figures or artwork? Will you be expected to prepare the indexes? If they are contracted out, who will pay for this work? Will your book include supplements (e.g., instructor's manual, test bank, transparencies, and study guide), and will you be expected to prepare them? Again, if they are contracted out, who will cover these expenses? How much will your book be sold for (which affects the amount you make on each copy)?—and many other such questions. Because these sorts of issues are not always obvious to novice textbook writers, it is a good idea to consult several successful authors in your department or elsewhere—and maybe even an attorney familiar with the publishing industry—for additional advice in this area.

This is *not* to imply that you should choose your publisher on the basis of the contract alone (assuming you have a choice). Rather, consider also how large and well-known the publisher is in psychology, how large a field staff they have, the other psychology books on their list (including any that may compete with yours), and so forth. It may be worth contacting one or more authors of current texts at these houses to learn how satisfied they have been with the production and marketing of their books. Finally, think about how you have previously been treated by the sales reps for each publisher. Have you seen them regularly? Do they follow through on their promises? Do they do an impressive job of presenting their products? Remember, it is these same reps who will potentially be going door-to-door with your book.

THE WRITING STAGE

Having successfully made your way through the educational system, you probably have the requisite wherewithal to handle the actual writing of a book—but it is still worth mentioning a few points briefly.

If you are not a reasonably well-organized person, in terms of both time and space, you probably should think twice about taking on a textbook.

The sheer enormity of the task almost demands a systematic approach along a number of dimensions. If your dissertation took an inordinate amount of time to set down in print (and there you were presumably writing on a topic about which you were already expert), consider what lies before you.

Time may be the biggest challenge. Day-to-day demands will always be there, so if you let them supplant your writing time, you are lost. It is clichéd to say that you must set aside inviolable time to work on the book, but then again, clichés are often accurate.

Space can also be important. It helps to have a place where materials can be spread out and left undisturbed until you return to the writing. Don't plan to work at your office desk in between visits by students and colleagues—find a place to hide.

The order in which you do the writing reflects personal preference to some degree, but other considerations may play some part in this decision. In most books, the material builds on the foundation of the early chapters, which would argue for preparing the book from beginning to end. However, first-time authors may discover that their style evolves as they go along. One common pattern is to include too much detail in the initial chapters, making them longer and denser than those that follow. Preparing chapters out of order can help even out this tendency across the book. Some authors prefer to begin with those chapters with which they are most conversant. This approach particularly makes sense with regard to the sample chapters you plan to submit. If being up-to-date is crucial, it may be wise to identify those chapters whose material is advancing most rapidly and save these until the final stage of writing.

Throughout the project, you will be maintaining contact with the publisher. As mentioned earlier, batches of completed chapters will usually be sent out for review and will thus provide some feedback for your subsequent writing. Your editor may also offer suggestions based on the reviewers' comments, and it is worth considering them, because editors at major houses tend to be very savvy people.

One of the more disillusioning aspects of the process, however, also may be encountered at this point in the project. Publishing being a very competitive business, the goals and priorities of your editor will probably not be precisely congruent with your own. Sometimes this disparity becomes evident in what you might view as issues of academic integrity. For example, a particular controversy may have many points of view that require a good deal of exposition to present—but the budgetary and market constraints associated with longer books may make it impossible for the editor to allow you free rein in covering such topics. Alternatively, there may be an area of research that you perhaps feel is outdated, poorly conceptualized, or whatever, and so you choose to ignore it—but if reviewers point out its absence, the editor may put pressure on you to override your reservations and cover the material. These sorts of disagreements need not be common on your project, and keeping in mind the different priorities of the academic and business worlds may help to minimize the frustration caused by such conflicts.

CONCLUSION

Much of the preceding discussion has urged caution, vigilance, and skepticism in making the decision to write a text. But the news is not all grim. Writing a textbook can be an exciting and rewarding experience. At the very least, you will learn a great deal about your subject area, the world of publishing, and yourself. And maybe you will even realize some of those goals involving fame and money. Many successful authors will tell you that if they had known how difficult the task was going to be when they began, they probably would not have written the first word. But they will also tell you, on the other hand, that they now have no regrets.

Writing a textbook, then, can bring a number of tangible and professional rewards. But perhaps the most satisfying is simply the feeling you get when you go to a conference and a colleague tells you, "I'm using your book and my class loves it." Yeah!

14

REVIEWING YOUR PEERS

The accuracy, importance, and value of our contributions to knowledge are judged not by a national board of advisors but by colleagues respected for their research and scholarship—that is, by our peers. Thus do I define peer review, the system that plays so great a part in our lives—first as we are the persons who are judged, and then as we are the ones who judge. Short of perfection as the system may be, up and down the land, we subscribe to it as better than any other proposed.

A request to review the work of your colleagues conveys a mark of distinction: It signifies not only that your peers recognize your competence but that they consider you capable of being open-minded and fair and as possessing the moral integrity not to take advantage of privileged information. In short, the request is a compliment to your intelligence, knowledge, and character. Not to abuse the confidence placed in you, keep vividly in mind that you are judging the work of a person who, like yourself, is hard-working, dedicated, and sensitive to criticism.

Demanding of time and effort as reviewing is, the work holds many rewards. In criticizing the work of another, you come to set ever more stringent standards for your own efforts. And although in reviewing the work of others—for publication, research support, hiring, or promotion—you are given a great deal of privileged information, what you gain in new knowledge is not yours to use until it enters the public domain. Circumspect attention to this possibility strengthens our moral behavior, and in the end may be peer reviewing's greatest reward.

REVIEWING JOURNAL ARTICLES

Here your task is twofold: to assess the manuscript's contribution to knowledge and to provide advice to the author(s) if the manuscript can be improved. For both tasks you need a broad knowledge of the field—which is obvious—and a benevolent attitude—which is not quite so obvious. Take a moment to remind yourself of how easy it is to find flaws even in first-rate reports published in well-refereed journals. Isn't that how we teach our students? Would that we could be as critical of our own! Then, no matter how differently you would have solved the problem, try to limit your review to how the authors chose to solve it and do not chide them for not doing what you think they should have done. Be gentle and be modest; reviewing is not the appropriate occasion for displaying one's own cleverness.

In evaluating a manuscript, you ask of another's work the same questions that guide you in conducting research. Here I cannot improve on the main questions set forth in the APA *Publication Manual* (1983):

> Is the research question significant, and is the work original and important? Have the instruments been demonstrated to have satisfactory reliability and validity? Are the outcome measures clearly related to the variables with which the investigation is concerned? Does the research design fully and unambiguously test the hypothesis? Are the subjects representative of the population to which generalizations are made? Did the research observe ethical standards in the treatment of subjects . . .? Is the research at an advanced enough stage to make the publication of results meaningful? (pp. 19–20)

Do not be surprised to find yourself spending many hours on the review. Read the manuscript through quickly, put it away for a day or so, then study it part by part, working backward and forward, and eventually working out such details as the degrees of freedom in the statistical analyses. Often you need a trip to the library to bring your knowledge of the topic up-to-date. Allow some days of reflection as you turn the matter over in your mind. Only then are you ready to write the review.

Reviews are written for an editor, but just as importantly, for the authors. Tell the authors early on of your regard for what they set out to do, and find some noteworthy characteristics of the work or the writing to remark on. Most manuscripts require revisions (Eichorn & VandenBos, 1985), and your task is to present the need for them in such a way that you help the authors to improve the manuscript or their future efforts. The style of your writing is everything; be critical, as necessary, but above all, be courteous and respectful. Put yourself in the authors' place and consider how you would react to the review you have just written.

Here I give an example of harsh, demeaning, and impertinent statements in a recent review of a manuscript I coauthored: "This paper is *very* poorly written with long and cumbersome phrases, obsessive attention to trivial and repetitive details. . . . Why on earth does this deserve space in a journal? . . . I suggest that [the authors] put their energies into something new and valuable." Well deserved or not, imagine the effect on a less-seasoned investigator! (Incidentally, we sent the manuscript to another journal and it was accepted.) To balance the account, I am still grateful, after almost 40 years, to the anonymous reviewer who, in approving one of my manuscripts, added that if the study were a PhD dissertation, I should so state. I took that suggestion as an enormous compliment, because the study was no more than a class project carried out in a semester!

Besides empirical reports, there are of course many other types of articles, all to be judged by individually appropriate criteria. Whatever the task, put it high on your agenda and try to be prompt. The authors are out there anxiously waiting to learn the fate of their work. Let us hope they will have reason, as you yourself have had on occasion, to thank the anonymous reviewer.

REVIEWING RESEARCH PROPOSALS

Here you are asked by an agency to judge a research proposal's worthiness of financial support. What is the likelihood that it will add to our store of knowledge or lead to new discoveries? Given the investigators' training, experience, and past achievements, are they capable of fulfilling its promise? Is the plan well designed, the budget appropriate, and the institutional support adequate? For younger investigators, place greater weight on their potential of achieving; and for all proposals, look with special favor on promises of originality and creativity. You are judging the merits of an individual proposal and serving as an ad hoc reviewer.

You may also be invited to join a panel that considers proposals in your general area of competence. Panels may be composed of 10 or more members who represent a large area of knowledge, each accomplished in a facet of that area. In contrast to serving as an ad hoc reviewer on a single proposal, reviewers on a panel experience a lively exchange of ideas from which you come to define your own view of research. These are stimulating experiences; the members develop a sense of camaraderie and become good friends.

So far I have been writing about appraising individual research reports. There are other types of proposals on which your advice will be sought, such as program projects, career development and fellowship awards, research training programs, and conferences. Differ as they do, they all present the same challenge: to assess their promise of future achievement.

LETTERS OF REFERENCE

All of us, at one time or another, have to write letters of reference; unlike accepting an invitation to review manuscripts or research proposals, writing such letters is a duty that cannot be denied. You could claim insufficient knowledge of the candidate, but when the search committee accompanies the request with a sheaf of the candidate's reprints and preprints, the claim evaporates.

In an informative letter, try to be specific about the candidate's professional experiences and personal characteristics in relation to the demands of the position, and shun the empty superlatives.

Writing these letters is often a pleasure, but sometimes it will try you sorely. You want the best for the candidate, but you also have a duty to your discipline and to the institution asking your judgment. What if you have reservations about the candidate's qualifications? You cannot out of cowardice fob off a poor candidate on an unsuspecting department. Have you an obligation to discuss the matter with the candidate? But then you begin to worry that your judgment may not be correct. Can you console yourself with the hope that the committee will discount your possible biases? The only help I can offer is for you to discuss the problem with a trusted colleague. Incidentally, I think that I cannot give you a more telling example of your effect on events outside your classroom.

CONCLUDING REMARKS

Peer review sometimes falls short of the mark. Reviewers on occasion disagree in judging the merits of research proposals (perhaps understandably, because the outcome is not predictable) and also in the reviewing of manuscripts. In fact, a recent study (Fiske & Fogg, 1990) found that, in the typical case, two reviews of the same paper had no critical points in common. Yet we believe that no other system is as capable on the average of making sound, impartial, and creative judgments as peer review—so nimble at accommodating different opinions, so agile at keeping pace with the march of progress.

Peer review accepted, I turn to your part in the system. What for you is a mark of esteem and an opportunity to exercise critical faculties (and display your own peerless standards!) is for the judged an ordeal of fire. On your review of their article, grant proposal, or worthiness of hiring or promotion hinges their sense of esteem, their experience of success or failure, their emotion of joy or despair that affects not only themselves but all those dear to them. Your intelligence acknowledged, and without denying that standards must be upheld, you must be honest and just and, at absolutely no personal gain, rise above all bias. Thus, your decision today on that article, grant proposal, or letter of testimony on your desk may be of more far-reaching consequence than any other task awaiting your attention.

15

SERVING THE PUBLIC INTEREST

Professors serve society in many ways and in many arenas. We talk to PTA meetings, serve on hospital boards and town councils, teach in policy institutes, testify in Congress on health and education bills, work with human rights groups worldwide, and volunteer in Head Start classes, to name but a few of our activities. So much are these activities part of the "everyday-ness" of our lives that we seldom stop to credit them as contributions to society.

"To give psychology away" is a popular slogan of the day, but inasmuch as we study and teach human behavior, we have always been giving it away, and could scarcely do otherwise. Indeed, Lewis P. Lipsitt (1991) found evidence in the 1924 APA *Directory* that some of our most famous professors were even then dealing with the real world of human behavior. To quote his account, "They helped create the Alpha Tests of World War I, or had something to do with the redesign of the cockpit control panel in a fighter plane, or consulted in schools, or designed studies to evaluate the usefulness of one kind of psychological intervention or another" (p. 4).

AS MEMBERS OF PROFESSIONAL SOCIETIES

Our professional societies are formally dedicated to serving the public interest, a dedication that you and I as members share and honor. For

173

example, the APA's purpose is to advance psychology as a science, as a profession, and as a means of promoting human welfare. In addition, Principle F: Social Responsibility of the APA's Ethical Principles (1992) states:

> Psychologists are aware of their professional and scientific responsibilities to the community and the society in which they work and live. They apply and make public their knowledge of psychology in order to contribute to human welfare. . . . They are encouraged to contribute a portion of their professional time for little or no personal advantage. (p. 1600)

Similarly, the APS (1992) includes among its purposes "to promote public understanding of psychological science and its applications . . . and to encourage the 'giving away' of psychology in the public interest" (p. 202).

For other evidence of a concern for the public interest, we need look no further than the several awards that the APA annually confers on its members for distinguished contributions to public service, to research in public policy, and to psychology in the public interest. In addition, the American Psychological Foundation yearly presents a gold medal to a psychologist for an "enduring contribution to the application of psychology in the public interest."

So much for generalities! How do we honor these principles? How are these high-minded statements translated into activities?

Our professional societies inform us of the need at home and abroad for what we have learned about human behavior. Articles in the *American Psychologist*'s "Psychology in the Public Forum" describe what is being done and what more should be done about such serious problems as the rehabilitation of offenders and the prevention of disease. But we want more than information, and to that end they alert us to how we can help legislators and governmental officials solve such problems. For example, the Society for Research in Child Development regularly distributes new findings on child development to the governmental officials who set policies for children and families, and its Washington office arranges for its members to meet these officials. The APA's Scientific Psychology Action Network (APA-SPAN) performs a similar service for APA members. In sum, our professional societies help us find the right desk for our letters, the right office for meeting with congressional staff, and the right congressional hearings for presenting our testimony.

THROUGH CAMPUS ORGANIZATIONS

Our colleges and universities take pride in the public service their professors render, and they value it as an important part of their mission.

On many campuses, professors and students channel their efforts through centers and institutes.

Of special interest are policy institutes. Multidisciplinary and campus-wide, they work with state and federal policymakers to meet the nation's educational, health, and social needs. They teach professors and students how to translate research findings into solutions for real-life problems. For example, what do we know about the causes of children's prematurely dropping out of school that a lawmaker could use in proposing a program to keep them in school longer? But, as Gallagher (1990) pointed out, makers of policy want the information now, whereas we, as scientists, always want more data and more time to reach a conclusion. Still, some data, when properly presented, might be useful, and how to find and present them are the skills the institutes practice and teach.

In still other centers and institutes, professors serve the needs of their state, sometimes especially those of its children and families. For example, at the University of Minnesota (Weinberg, Fishhaut, Moore, & Plaisance, 1990), Michigan State University, and the University of Pittsburgh (McCall, 1990), faculty members from many disciplines bring the latest research findings to the attention of teachers, nurses, doctors, public health workers, and law enforcement officers, among others. They also teach continuing education courses, organize conferences, and sponsor workshop and training programs, thereby creating links between the research resources of a school and the needs of professionals in the field.

AS INDIVIDUALS

When you testify in Congress as a member of your professional society or help a school principal as a member of a policy institute, you are of course serving as an individual, but many of a professor's public services are performed independently of any supporting organization. When we serve thus, as individuals in our own right, we come close to the very persons whose behavior we study, who also are those who support us and deserve our efforts. Not only are they entitled to know the results of our labors and, what is probably even more important, how we obtain them, but what we know may be useful for their personal lives and for them as citizens concerned with social issues. Even without such good reasons, many of us are eager to tell the world what we know. Thus, we talk to lay groups, respond to the queries of reporters from the media, write for newspapers and magazines, and publish books of advice.

For some of us, responding to queries from journalists is worrisome. Might we be misquoted? Will they omit the qualifiers we deem so important? Will our profound thoughts, when processed through the journalist's computer, strike our colleagues as vacuous? But help is available (McCall, 1988).

Some campus news bureaus offer assistance. The APA's Division 46 (Media Psychology) also regularly presents workshops on how to communicate the ins and outs of research to the media; the notice for a recent workshop bore the startling title, "*USA Today* Is on the Phone: What Next?" (*Psychological Science Agenda*, 1992, 5, 16). In addition, the Media Referral Service of the APA's Public Affairs Office publishes two guides, "Handling the Media Interview: A Guide for Psychologists" and "Some Questions and Answers about Dealing with the Media: A Guide for Psychologists," available for the asking. You may also register with the service if you are willing to respond to the media's requests—of course, within your area of specialization. In fact, because of the Service's increasing popularity with the media, more volunteers are needed.

AS CITIZENS OF THE WORLD

As professors, we are human beings first and educated professionals second. Indeed, the AAUP 1940 Statement of Principles on Academic Freedom and Tenure (1990b) puts it thus: "College and university teachers are citizens, members of a learned profession, and officers of an educational institution" (p. 4). As members of a learned profession, that is as psychologists, we have long been concerned with the welfare of humankind.

In the first instance, I refer to another major principle of the APA (1992) code of ethics, Principle D: Respect for People's Rights and Dignity, the first sentence of which declares, "Psychologists accord appropriate respect to the fundamental rights, dignity, and worth of all people" (p. 1599). This principle has long been part of our published code, and over the years, the APA Council has passed resolution after resolution in support of human rights (Rosenzweig, 1988). A recent section in the *American Psychologist*'s Public Forum on "The Rights of the Child" urges us to lend our efforts to the worldwide observance of these rights as adopted by the United Nations Convention in 1989.

Other professional organizations also monitor the observing of human rights. For example, since 1976, AAAS has monitored the actions of governments worldwide that circumscribe the freedom of scientists; its Committee on Scientific Freedom and Responsibility reports annually on the plight of scientists, engineers, and health professionals whose human rights have been violated or whose academic freedom has been restricted. In particular, its Science and Human Rights Program (1992) recommends that we, as well as our scientific societies, express our concerns to the governments of the oppressed persons, in this respect mirroring the successful letter-writing campaigns of Amnesty International.

Let us acknowledge, furthermore, that the welfare of humankind hinges on the welfare of the environment; it is past time to curb human activities that deplete the earth's physical and biological resources. In the end, every problem of our universe involves human behavior—as cause or as cure—and it is precisely here that psychology plays the significant role.

To return to the AAUP statement, as both citizens and educated professionals we carry special responsibilities for the welfare of people everywhere. We move outside the classroom and laboratory to serve the public interests of our communities, the state, the nation, and the world. We come at last to where we began: In the "giving away" of what we have learned, we fulfill George Miller's (1969) vision of psychology as a means of promoting human welfare.

16

THE ACTUAL AND THE POSSIBLE

As we mature and settle into a routine, the actual—the here and now—fills our days, often with little room for the possible, the possible that looks ahead and, in François Jacob's (1982) words, "invents the future" (p. 54). Not only do the day's chores and responsibilities clamor for attention but they bid fair to use up all the available time and energy, while dreams of the future recede into the distance—just the reverse of how matters stood when we were young and the enormity of the possible left us breathless.

Of course, the actual contains more than our professional activities. Even as we carry them with us when away from our desks, we are also engaged in a personal life in the larger world. Like everyone else, we, too, have family pleasures and responsibilities, interests in sports, literature, music, and all the arts, as well as civic and church responsibilities, to say nothing of the chores of daily living, of keeping ourselves and our families fed and warm, in sickness and in health, with transportation for all in automobiles that run on demand. How then can we do justice to the demands of the present—our professional as well as our personal, social, and civic duties—while entertaining thoughts of the possible?

Now I am beset by conflicting ideas. In the first place, only a little thought takes me to the obvious: Just as today's actual was yesterday's possible, so will today's possible become tomorrow's actual. And so I see that the actual does in fact hold many of yesterday's fulfilled dreams. Indeed, as we accomplish the possible, lo and behold, it becomes the actual! Attracted as I am to the possible, even as I contemplate it, it slips from my grasp.

Still, if you are teased by dreams not yet realized, I suggest some ways by which you can fulfill them, or at least by which you can enliven the actual, even if only in the contemplating. Indeed, the possible can add the measure of excitement that comes from tackling a new problem, now that we know so well how to handle the actual. So, perhaps, when the actual becomes routine, it may be time to envision the possible.

All the possibles I outline here have been covered in earlier chapters, but now, placed in a different context, they acquire a tinge of novelty and merit a fresh look.

KEEPING INFORMED

To keep abreast of new knowledge presents itself as a possible, but it is one that day by day we transform into the actual because ours is a profession in which we do not, indeed cannot, stand still. The more we learn, the more we discern how much more there is to learn. As John Donne so aptly wrote, "The greater the island of knowledge, the longer the shoreline of the unknown."

Here I am reminded of the 1986 adjustments made by the world's measurement laboratories to the established physical constants. Although a constant is something that is supposed never to change, an international coalition of scientists changed more than 100 of the fundamental constants on which the work of science depends. For example, the new standard for the speed of light changes the heretofore standard definition of a meter. If the length of a meter can be revised, I echo the title of the *New York Times* article (Browne, 1987) on the new constants to ask, "Is Nothing Sacred?"

Nothing in scholarship or science *is* sacred. Overnight, new discoveries are made, new theories are proposed, new disciplines arise and old ones are redefined. Indeed, new knowledge changes even the accepted canon of facts and principles. Could Bentley Glass be right? He proposed (1985) that what we know in science depreciates at the same rate as an automobile—that is, in 5 to 8 years. (At this point in the margin of my copy, I wrote "Good grief!") Nor can we anticipate with equanimity knowing less than our students about some newly developed theory or technique. Then, as we cannot read everything in today's avalanche of information, we perforce must limit ourselves to a chosen few books and journals, and sometimes only to skimming them until our heads reel.

Instead, to keep you in the forefront of knowledge I suggest some activities that fortunately do not take enormous amounts of time and, with a little planning, can be fitted into the daily routine. For example, advising colleagues on the manuscripts and grant proposals they are planning to submit carries you to the edge of new knowledge. You would also be a welcomed volunteer to your department's ethical review committee where, in reviewing the proposed new studies of the faculty, you are also carried into the future. Note, too, that many journals call for volunteer reviewers; and certainly such reviewing keeps you informed, as does writing a book review. Last, lose no opportunity to attend colloquia—even outside your own department. I have presented scarcely a new suggestion—these are activities you engage in often—but I have changed their import: They are indeed avenues to achieving the possible of keeping informed.

IMPROVING YOUR MIND

In 1933, Franklin D. Roosevelt, a few days after his inauguration, called on Justice Oliver Wendell Holmes and found him reading Plato. Roosevelt asked, "Why do you read Plato, Mr. Justice?" "To improve my mind, Mr. President," Holmes replied (Bowen, 1944, p. 414). Holmes was then 92 years old! I trust that this story takes the edge off this section's heading.

Rather than reading Plato, professors can effect a similar result by creating new syntheses of knowledge—another set of possibles. Designing a new course of instruction would be such an achievement. As new facts come to our attention, as yesterday's theories are amended, and as different social problems arise to vex us, a rearranging of knowledge can provide timely instruction. Other syntheses can be developed by reviewing and organizing the rapidly expanding body of our scientific literature. We are sorely in need of such efforts; you would perform a great service to all of us, and undoubtedly with gain to yourself, by discovering hitherto unremarked relationships. Another kind of synthesis could result from organizing a conference on an interesting and important topic, bringing together participants holding diverse points of view, this time for the purpose of exploring areas of agreement (often a more difficult and valuable exercise then finding differences).

We can also improve our minds by viewing the place of our everyday efforts in the classroom, the library, and the laboratory in the larger world of endeavors. Near at hand are possibilities of serving on faculty committees that work to solve campus-wide problems, and you can thus step outside the parochialism of your own discipline. Beyond the campus lie a score of community organizations that welcome your services. To see the relevance of your professional knowledge and skills to the problems of, for example, schools, hospitals, rest homes, and prisons is rewarding, even as it extends the boundaries of your life.

You can move even farther away to gain still other perspectives. You can accept an invitation to teach on another campus. Yes, you can plan to teach the same old course, but it will become a different course as you teach it to students drawn from a different population and as you interact with different colleagues. To teaching on another campus I can add working in a colleague's laboratory on problems you cannot fit into your usual schedule or working in an interdisciplinary research or social policy institute, as well as being a congressional fellow in the legislative or executive branches of the government.

Granted, no possible I propose may equal the effect of reading Plato in improving your mind. There is nothing wrong with reading Plato (after all, I was a philosophy major at Cornell), but here it seems a bit off the mark.

PAUSING TO THINK

Can you program a time to sit in stillness and think, to empty your mind of daily busyness until a great idea falls into it? How much quiet time do you need? And how productive will it be?

Shortly after Einstein settled in the United States, he is said to have plaintively commented on the unquiet atmosphere of academe (in Princeton, no less!) and its deleterious effect on scientific productivity (Ginsberg, 1962, p. 1305). And Bertrand Russell (Russell, 1969) warned that "it is not by bustle that men become enlightened. Spinoza was content with the Hague; Kant, who is generally regarded as the wisest of Germans, never traveled more than 10 miles from Königsberg." But we are not Einstein, Spinoza, or Kant, and so we probably need even more quiet time. Yet I question the implication that putting your brain in neutral will automatically provide great insights. Certainly we can stop to take stock of what we are doing and to ponder how best to deploy our talents, and perhaps thereby we will gain a new vision of the sense of our efforts. Let us recognize, however, that a perception of the essential meaning of our work, an intuitive grasp of reality, can—and often does—arise in the midst of daily labors.

On reflection (note!), I have come to the conclusion that we probably cannot think on command, that we cannot say that in this hour we will conjure up a great thought. No, the prized insight slips in quietly and, like Sandburg's fog, on little cat feet. But if we cannot set aside time just to think, we can take time to be careful, to be accurate, and to avoid the foolish and the shallow.

OF TIME, MONEY, AND PLANS

To move beyond the demands of the day, you need time (that most precious of commodities), perhaps a place apart from those demands, and often money—for all of which you need a plan. Let us then start with plans, ever aware that just to plan takes time.

When do you start to plan? Now! And how do you start? Designate one of your desk drawers as the repository of possibles. Drop into it announcements of conferences, grants, lectureships, invitations, workshops, meetings, requests for research proposals, notices of fellowships, calls for volunteers, and so on, as they come to your attention. Whenever the present is too much with you, spend some moments sorting and re-sorting the contents of the drawer into "maybe" and "for sure," "close at hand" and "far away," and so on. Then, the present—the actual—recedes, as the future—the possible—beckons. Of course, for you, a computer file might serve as well as a drawer.

To secure any large block of time, even at home, takes planning and time. Not to disappoint yourself, increase by my factor of four the amount of time you think you need to arrange for a leave, to submit a course of study and research if leaves are competitive, and to apply to a foundation or governmental agency for financial support. And then you may need as much as a year to work out arrangements with your own and the host institution, to find substitutes for your classes, and to plan the progress of your students.

I reserve for the last the most difficult: family arrangements. The care of your home in your absence is the least of them. If you are married, can your spouse's needs be accommodated or career served? If you have children, can their schooling be interrupted, and would the new site offer them compensatory gains? Even with your children grown and away from home, a leave may not be convenient. For example, when I was invited to spend a year at the Center for Advanced Study in the Behavioral Sciences at Palo Alto, I was able to go for only one month: My husband could not leave his academic duties, and I was responsible for the care of my mother. Short as the time was, however, it was there that I found the tranquillity to read a few books from cover to cover, profited by meeting new colleagues, and, best of all, experienced the flash of insight that I describe in the section that follows.

CHERISHING YOUR OWN INSIGHTS

There is much about the academic life to humble a person. When you are a student, your professors know so much more than you; your fellow students are as eager to learn, as dedicated and hard-working as you; and always far above you are the brilliant achievements of the great thinkers in your field. Then, later, when you are that professor who knows so much, how humbling it is to know how little that "much" really is. All the more reason, then, when we suddenly have an idea that illumines the world around us, to pause and cherish it.

As often as I have thought of writing these paragraphs, just as often have I ruled them out as trivial and self-indulgent. But, on balance, I now judge my advice on cherishing our own insights to be worthy of your attention. We have been so sternly taught to document the source of every thought that we tremble to declare an insight as ours. No matter that tomorrow you may find that some (other?) genius preceded you, rejoice at the moment you glimpse a "truth." Never mind that all those ideas may wither away; the emotion uplifts.

Insights do not come often. They cannot be called up on command. They do not always come when you are reading or writing or talking, but rather catch you in a moment of reverie. Each comes unbidden, appearing as a great discovery and, as it lights the world around you, you become aware of exactly where you are—the time and the place—a memory forever associated with the insight. I presume to consider that these insights qualify as epiphanies.

I write of two that now give me even more pleasure in remembering than I permitted myself at their birth. One night in 1958 I could not sleep but tossed and turned until dawn, as I was struck by the great idea that even 3-month-old infants were already active participants of life, that they were not passive and consumed only by oral needs, as the literature had portrayed. Today, that insight seems paltry, even to me, but its occurrence is as vivid today as it was that night more than 30 years ago. It seemed so important to me then that at the meetings of the Society for Research in Child Development the following spring, I read a paper in which I challenged the relevant Freudian doctrine. The yellowed and brittle newspaper account of that presentation recently turned up among my papers; I read it with great pleasure, and in fact it presented the stimulus for writing these words.

The second insight occurred in 1967 during my stay at the Center for Advanced Study in the Behavioral Sciences. In an office not cluttered with a career's accumulation of books, journals, reprints, book ads, students' papers, and research data—all demanding immediate attention—I suddenly glimpsed what seemed to be the essential meaning of a laboratory study Carol Eckerman and I had just finished in Chapel Hill. We had shown that crawling infants left their mothers sooner when there were toys in an adjoining room than when there were none. But the insight that stunned me, in that quiet study away from home, was that the infants would leave their mothers and enter a room without toys, that is, an *empty* room. Contrary to the ethos of the times, not only did these infants not cling to their mothers in an unfamiliar environment but, like free spirits, out on their own, they were ready to find out what the next room in the lab—a room with a bare floor, bare walls, and no furniture—might offer their curiosity.

Personal testimony aside, I do not regard these insights—and a few others I have had—as important discoveries; rather, it is the elation of an insight that I write about. But, whether it was a great insight, or whether you were the first to have it, time takes care of putting it in its proper place—and you, as well. Nevertheless, I believe we are entitled to each glow while it lasts and to recall them all warmly over the years.

EPILOGUE:
ONCE OVER, LIGHTLY

I began this book bravely, as though I knew whereof I would write. As I now reread my words, I worry that I may have written no more than a personal statement of the goals and standards of our profession. However imperfectly I may have realized them, I continue to have faith in their underlying value and commend them to your attention.

Now, too, I see how much emphasis these pages place on work—lots of it. But work need not be grim; exacting and conscientious as it must be, it can be exhilarating and gratifying. Would that all of us could say what Judge Edward Weinfeld, a few years before retiring from the bench at the age of 86, wrote of his attitude toward his work:

> When, at a fairly early hour of the morning [he regularly arrived at the courthouse before 6:00 AM], I put the key into the door of my darkened chambers and walk across the room to start the day's activities, I do so with the same enthusiasm that was mine the very first day of my judicial career. What one enjoys is not work. It is joy. (Lubasch, 1988)

In writing these pages, I meant only to teach but was surprised, as I should not have been, to find that I also learned. I saw, as though for the first time, the freedom and power of our professional lives and gained some new insights into our activities.

In the first instance, we live a professional life in which all our activities complement one another. From the years of graduate study to the years of service, a common set of values guides our efforts. To read and to evaluate a piece of writing provide criteria not only for our own writing, but also for judging the writing of others, as well as for teaching our students. The rules governing the scientific enterprise not only inform our own efforts, but also provide the standards by which we judge the work of others, as well as those that we inculcate in our students. What we learned as graduate students inspired a life of scholarship, and from a life of teaching, writing, and inquiring, we learn how to bring up another generation of scholars. And as we become more sensitive to the ethical standards governing our behavior as teachers, scholars, and investigators, we become ever more conscious of their importance in guiding our own and our students' behavior. Thus, what is learned in one context serves performance in another, and in performing, we continue to learn. Ours is truly a life of learning how better to serve our ideals.

So, too, was I impressed anew by the power that academic freedom grants us. It is to the rule of academic freedom that we owe the right to speak freely without penalty—that is, to present our discipline to our students as we deem proper, to write on topics of our own choice, and to investigate what we consider important. And our authority does not end there, for as reviewers of our peers, we appraise the merits of their efforts to contribute to knowledge. Furthermore, in collegial self-government, we control academic matters by establishing the course of study, choosing our colleagues, and determining the reputation of our discipline within the institution, and of the institution in the eyes of the world. As UNC chancellor Christopher C. Fordham said in 1987, the faculty are the mind, heart, and soul of the institution.

Finally, these insights aroused in me a sense of wonder and reverence for the system in which we live and work. The power that is ours demands adherence to the highest principles of personal integrity and honor, to wisdom, fairness, and a deep concern for the rights and needs of others. Only by behaving responsibly in discharging our obligation to the society that sustains us can we ensure the continuing of such freedom.

Stern mentor though I have been, at the end let me confess that here, and throughout my life, I have tried to do more than I knew how to do, and that with age and experience the task gets no easier and the challenge remains. Yet I am vain enough to view that as the common condition of creators and transmitters of knowledge, fortunately a condition that keeps us from being arrogant. To realize our aspirations, and here I paraphrase Lawrence A. Kimpton's tribute to the University of Chicago at the June 1960 Convocation, we are forever innovating and therefore forever inquisitive in mind, adventurous in spirit, and young of heart. By these words to you, I discharge in some small measure my debt to my alma maters, my mentors, and my students.

REFERENCES

Abramovitch, R., Freedman, J. L., Thoden, K., & Nikolich, C. (1991). Children's capacity to consent to participation in psychological research: Empirical findings. *Child Development, 62,* 1100–1109.

Adams, H. B. (1931). *The education of Henry Adams.* New York: Modern Library.

Albee, G. W. (1984). On honoraria. *American Psychologist, 39,* 1487–1491.

American Association for the Advancement of Science. (1990). Resolution on the use of animals in research, testing, and education. *Science, 250,* 611.

American Association for the Advancement of Science–American Bar Association National Conference of Lawyers and Scientists. (1989). *Project on Scientific Fraud and Misconduct, Report on Workshop Number Three.* Washington, DC: American Association for the Advancement of Science.

American Association for the Advancement of Science, Science and Human Rights Program. (1992). *Directory of persecuted scientists, engineers, and health professionals.* Washington, DC: Author.

American Association of University Professors. (1990a). Joint statement on government of colleges and universities. *Policy documents and reports* (pp. 119–124). Washington, DC: Author.

American Association of University Professors. (1990b). 1940 Statement of principles on academic freedom and tenure. *Policy documents and reports* (pp. 3–4). Washington, DC: Author.

American Association of University Professors. (1990c). Statement on teaching evaluations. *Policy documents and reports* (pp. 167–170). Washington, DC: Author.

American Psychological Association. (1983). *Publication manual of the American Psychological Association* (3rd ed.). Washington, DC: Author.

American Psychological Association. (1985). *Guidelines for ethical conduct in the care and use of animals.* Washington, DC: Author.

American Psychological Association. (1990). *Directory of ethnic minority professionals in psychology* (2nd ed.). Washington, DC: Author.

American Psychological Association. (1992). Ethical principles of psychologists and code of conduct. *American Psychologist, 47,* 1597–1611.

American Psychological Association. (1993). *Journals in psychology: A resource listing for authors* (4th ed.). Washington, DC: Author.

American Psychological Association, Committee on Women in Psychology. (1992). *Survival guide to academia for women and ethnic minorities.* Washington, DC: Author.

American Psychological Association, Committee on Women in Psychology and

Women's Program Office. (1988). *Understanding the manuscript review process: Increasing the participation of women* (3rd ed.). Washington, DC: Author.

American Psychological Society. (1992). *Psychological Science, 3,* 202.

Angell, J. R. (1936). James Rowland Angell. In C. Murchison (Ed.), *A history of psychology in autobiography* (Vol. 3, pp. 3–29). Worcester, MA: Clark University Press.

Animal Behavior Society. (1986). Guidelines for the use of animals in research. *Animal Behaviour, 34,* 315–318.

Babbage, C. (1971). *Reflections on the decline of science in England, and on some of its causes.* Shannon, Ireland: Irish University Press. (Original work published 1830)

Babkin, B. P. (1949). *Pavlov, a biography.* Chicago: University of Chicago Press.

Barzun, J. (1983). William James, author. *American Scholar, 52,* 41–48.

Benjamin, L. T., Jr., & Lowman, K. D. (Eds.). (1981). *Activities handbook for the teaching of psychology* (Vol. 1). Washington, DC: American Psychological Association.

Blass, E. (1991). Professionalism and academia. In R. R. Kilburg (Ed.), *How to manage your career in psychology* (pp. 125–141). Washington, DC: American Psychological Association.

Bowen, D. C. (1944). *Yankee from Olympus: Justice Holmes and his family.* Boston: Little, Brown.

Bridgwater, C. A., Bornstein, P. H., & Walkenbach, J. (1981). Ethical issues and the assignment of publication credit. *American Psychologist, 36,* 524–525.

Broad, W., & Wade, N. (1982). *Betrayers of the truth.* New York: Simon & Schuster.

Browne, M. W. (1987, February 24). Is nothing sacred? Constants of science submit to revision. *The New York Times,* p. C3.

Buhite, R. D., & Levy, D. W. (Eds.). (1992). *FDR's fireside chats.* Norman, OK: University of Oklahoma Press.

Carr, H. A. (1936). Harvey A. Carr. In C. F. Murchison (Ed.), *A history of psychology in autobiography* (Vol. 3, pp. 69–82). Worcester, MA: Clark University Press.

Chamberlin, T. C. (1965). The method of multiple working hypotheses. *Science, 148,* 754–759. (Original work published 1890)

Cobbett, W. (1980). *Advice to young men, and (incidentally) to young women.* Oxford: Oxford University Press. (Original work published 1830)

Cohen, J. (1990). Things I have learned (so far). *American Psychologist, 45,* 1304–1312.

Cole, J. R., & Luckerman, H. (1987). Marriage, motherhood and research performance in science. *Scientific American, 256,* 119–125.

Cone, J. D., & Foster, S. L. (1993). *Dissertations and theses from start to finish: Psychology and related fields.* Washington, DC: American Psychological Association.

Cuthill, I. (1991). Field experiments in animal behaviour: Methods and ethics. *Animal Behaviour, 42,* 1007–1014.

Darley, J. M., & Zanna, M. P. (1987). The hiring process in academia. In M. P. Zanna & J. M. Darley (Eds.), *The compleat academic: A practical guide for the beginning social scientist* (pp. 3–20). New York: Random House.

Dewsbury, D. A. (1990). Early interactions between animal psychologists and animal activists and the founding of the APA Committee on Precautions in Animal Experimentation. *American Psychologist, 45,* 315–327.

Eble, K. E. (1983). *The aims of college teaching.* San Francisco: Jossey-Bass.

Eichorn, D. H., & VandenBos, G. R. (1985). Dissemination of scientific and professional knowledge: Journal publication with the APA. *American Psychologist, 40,* 1309–1316.

Epstein, J. (Ed.). (1981). *Masters: Portraits of great teachers.* New York: Basic Books.

Everitt, B. S., & Hay, D. F. (1992). *Talking about statistics: A psychologist's guide to data analysis.* New York: John Wiley & Sons, Halsted Press.

Fellman, D. (1973). Academic freedom. In P. P. Wiener (Ed.), *Dictionary of the history of ideas: Studies of selected pivotal ideas* (Vol. 1, pp. 9–17). New York: Scribner's.

Fiske, D. W., & Fogg, L. (1990). But the reviewers are making different criticisms of my paper! *American Psychologist, 45,* 591–598.

Fleischer, J. (1986, September 29). Working for college keeps new dean booked. *The Daily Tar Heel,* pp. 1, 3.

Fowler, H. W. (1926). *A dictionary of modern English usage.* Oxford: Clarendon Press.

Gallagher, J. J. (1990). Emergence of policy studies and policy institutes. *American Psychologist, 45,* 1316–1318.

Ginsberg, E. (1962). Time and talent. *Science, 138,* 1305.

Glass, B. (1985). *Progress or catastrophe: The nature of biological science and its impact on human society.* New York: Praeger.

Gleckner, R. F. (1988). A taxonomy of colleges and universities. In A. L. Deneef, C. D. Goodwin, & E. S. McCrate (Eds.), *The academic's handbook* (pp. 4–18). Durham, NC: Duke University Press.

Gleitman, H. (1984). Introducing psychology. *American Psychologist, 39,* 421–427.

Grisso, T., Baldwin, E., Blanck, P. D., Rotheram-Borus, M. J., Schooler, N. R., & Thompson, T. (1991). Standards in research: APA's mechanism for monitoring the challenges. *American Psychologist, 46,* 758–766.

Hartley, J. (1991). Tabling information. *American Psychologist, 46,* 655–656.

Hayes, L. J., & Hayes, S. C. (1989). Writing your vita. *APS Observer, 2,* 15–17.

Herring, K. L. (1987). *APA's guide to research support* (3rd ed.). Washington, DC: American Psychological Association.

Hofstadter, R., & Metzger, W. P. (1955). *The development of academic freedom in the United States.* New York: Columbia University Press.

Holton, G. (1986). Niels Bohr and the integrity of science. *American Scientist, 74,* 237–243.

Hull, C. L. (1952). Clark L. Hull. In E. G. Boring, H. S. Langfeld, H. Werner, & R. M. Yerkes (Eds.), *A history of psychology in autobiography* (Vol. 4, pp. 143–162). Worcester, MA: Clark University Press.

Jacob, F. (1982). *The possible and the actual.* Seattle, WA: University of Washington Press.

Kaplan, A. (1964). *The conduct of inquiry: Methodology for behavioral science.* Scranton, PA: Chandler.

Kasarda, J. D. (1985). *The research mission of the University of North Carolina at Chapel Hill.* Chapel Hill: University of North Carolina, Self-Study Steering Committee.

Lipsitt, L. P. (1991). From the Executive Director: "Ancients" were both basic and applied psychologists. *Psychological Science Agenda, 4,* 4.

Lowman, J. (1984). *Mastering the techniques of teaching.* San Francisco: Jossey-Bass.

Lubasch, A. H. (1988, January 18). Judge Edward Weinfeld, 86, dies; on U.S. bench nearly 4 decades. *The New York Times,* p. 18.

Makosky, V. P., Sileo, C. C., Whittemore, L. G., Landry, C. P., & Skutley, M. L. (Eds.). (1990). *Activities handbook for the teaching of psychology* (Vol. 3). Washington, DC: American Psychological Association.

Makosky, V. P., Whittemore, L. G., & Rogers, A. M. (Eds.). (1988). *Activities handbook for the teaching of psychology* (Vol. 2). Washington, DC: American Psychological Association.

McCall, R. B. (1988). Science and the press: *Like oil and water? American Psychologist, 43,* 87–94.

McCall, R. B. (1990). Promoting interdisciplinary and faculty–service–provider relations. *American Psychologist, 45,* 1319–1324.

McKay, N. Y. (1988). Minority faculty in [mainstream white] academia. In A. L. Deneef, C. D. Goodwin, & E. S. McCrate (Eds.), *The academic's handbook* (pp. 46–60). Durham, NC: Duke University Press.

McKeachie, W. J. (1986). *Teaching tips* (8th ed.). Lexington, MA: Heath.

Medawar, P. B. (1979). *Advice to a young scientist.* New York: Harper & Row.

Miller, G. A. (1969). Psychology as a means of promoting human welfare. *American Psychologist, 24,* 1063–1075.

Miller, N. E. (1983). Behavioral medicine: Symbiosis between laboratory and clinic. *Annual review of psychology* (Vol. 38, pp. 1–31). Palo Alto, CA: Annual Reviews.

Morrow, J. R. (1968). Academic freedom. In D. L. Sills (Ed.), *International encyclopedia of the social sciences* (Vol. 1, pp. 4–10). New York: Macmillan and the Free Press.

National Academy of Sciences, Committee on the Conduct of Science. (1989). *On being a scientist.* Washington, DC: National Academy Press.

National Commission for Protection of Human Subjects of Biomedical and Behavioral Research. (1979). *The Belmont report: Ethical principles and guidelines for the protection of human subjects of research* (DHEW Publication No. OS78-0013). Washington, DC: Author.

O'Connor, M. (1979). *The scientist as editor.* New York: Wiley.

O'Connor, M., & Woodford, F. P. (1975). *Writing scientific papers in English, an ELSE-Ciba Foundation guide for authors.* Amsterdam: Elsevier.

Pelikan, J. (1983). *Scholarship and its survival.* Princeton, NJ: Carnegie Foundation for the Advancement of Teaching.

Platt, J. R. (1964). Strong inference. *Science, 146,* 347–353.

Pritchett, V. S. (1981, January 19). A study of delight. *The New Yorker,* p. 109.

Pye, A. K. (1988). University governance and autonomy–Who decides what in the university. In A. L. Deneef, C. D. Goodwin, & E. S. McCrate (Eds.), *The academic's handbook* (pp. 241–259). Durham, NC: Duke University Press.

Rheingold, H. L. (1961). The effect of environmental stimulation upon social and exploratory behavior in the human infant. In B. M. Foss (Ed.), *Determinants of infant behaviour* (pp. 143–171). London: Methuen.

Rheingold, H. L. (1963). Controlling the infant's exploratory behavior. In B. M. Foss (Ed.), *Determinants of infant behaviour II* (pp. 171–178). London: Methuen.

Rheingold, H. L. (1969). The effect of a strange environment on the behavior of infants. In B. M. Foss (Ed.), *Determinants of infant behaviour IV* (pp. 137–166). London: Methuen.

Rheingold, H. L. (1982). Ethics as an integral part of research in child development. In R. Vasta (Ed.), *Strategies and techniques of child study* (pp. 305–324). New York: Academic Press.

Rheingold, H. L., & Keene, G. C. (1965). Transport of the human young. In B. M. Foss (Ed.), *Determinants of infant behaviour III* (pp. 316–326). London: Methuen.

Rose, P. (1983). *Parallel lives.* New York: Knopf.

Rosenzweig, M. R. (1988). Psychology and United Nations human rights efforts. *American Psychologist, 43,* 79–86.

Russell, B. (1969, July 16). Lord Russell: 'Let's stay off the moon.' *The Wall Street Journal,* p. A16.

Russo, N. F., & Denmark, F. L. (1987). Contributions of women to psychology. In M. R. Rosenzweig & L. W. Porter (Eds.), *Annual Review of Psychology* (Vol. 38, pp. 279–298). Palo Alto: Annual Reviews.

Selye, H. (1964). *From dream to discovery: On being a scientist.* New York: McGraw-Hill.

Sigma Xi. (1984). *Honor in science.* New Haven, CT: Author.

Sigma Xi. (1987). *A new agenda for science.* New Haven, CT: Author.

Sigma Xi, Committee on Science and Society. (1991). Sigma Xi statement on the use of animals in research. *American Scientist, 80,* 73–76.

Silva, F. (1985, November 30). Popular UNC law professor retiring from full-time duty. *The News and Observer,* Raleigh, NC, p. 1C.

Sindermann, C. J. (1982). *Winning the games scientists play.* New York: Plenum.

Society for Research in Child Development. (1990, Winter). Ethical standards for research with children. *Newsletter,* pp. 5–7.

Spiegel, D., & Keith-Spiegel, P. (1970). Assignment of publication credits: Ethics and practices of psychologists. *American Psychologist, 25,* 738–747.

Steinbeck, J. (1969). *Journal of a novel: The East of Eden letters.* New York: Viking.

Steinberg, J., & Kennedy, C. (1991). Writing successful grant applications. *APS Observer, 4,* 1–4.

Stricker, G., Davis-Russell, E., Bourg, E., Duran, E., Hammond, W. R., McHolland, J., Polite, K., & Vaughn, B. E. (Eds.). (1990). *Toward ethnic diversification in psychology education and training.* Washington, DC: American Psychological Association.

Strunk, W., Jr., & White, E. B. (1959). *The elements of style.* New York: Macmillan.

Szent-Györgi, A. (1971). Looking back. *Perspectives in Biology and Medicine, 15,* 1–6.

Thorndike, E. L. (1898). Animal intelligence: An experimental study of the associative processes in animals. *Psychological Review Monographs, 2* (4, Whole No. 8).

Tufte, E. R. (1983). *The visual display of quantitative information.* Cheshire, CT: Graphics Press.

Tufte, E. R. (1990). *Envisioning information.* Cheshire, CT: Graphics Press.

Underwood, B. J. (1957). *Psychological research.* New York: Appleton-Century-Crofts.

U.S. Congress, Office of Technology Assessment. (1986). *Alternatives to animal use in research, testing, and education.* Washington, DC: U.S. Government Printing Office.

Weinberg, R. A., Fishhaut, E. H., Moore, S. G., & Plaisance, C. (1990). The Center for Early Education and Development: "Giving away" child psychology. *American Psychologist, 45,* 1325–1328.

Weiser, M. (1991). The computer for the 21st century. *Scientific American, 265,* 94–104.

Whitehead, A. N. (1957). *The aims of education.* New York: Macmillan. (Original work published 1929)

Wilbur, H. M. (1988). On getting a job. In A. L. Deneef, C. D. Goodwin, & E. S. McCrate (Eds.), *The academic's handbook* (pp. 63–76). Durham, NC: Duke University Press.

Williams, J. M. (1990). *Style: Toward clarity and grace.* Chicago: University of Chicago Press.

Young, P. T. (1928). Precautions in animal experimentation. *Psychological Bulletin, 35,* 487–489.

INDEX

serving on, value of, 94, 144, 181
types of
    academic criteria, 145
    animal care standards, 62
    hiring and promotion, 18, 91–92, 145
    student examining, 29, 41, 45–46
Community of scholars
    colleagues
        as advisors, 130, 137, 138
        reviewing work of, 167–171
    collegiality, 27–28, 30–31
Computers, 62, 78–79, 119, 139
Cone, J. D., 9
Conferences
    organizing, 157–158, 181
    participating in, 156–157
Contemplation, finding time for, 119, 182–
    183
Conventions, professional. See Meetings,
    professional
Cornell University, 7, 30, 75
Credit, intellectual, 8, 52. See also Coau-
    thorship: credit for
Curie, Marie, 75
Curie, Pierre, 75
Curriculum vitae, 16–17, 135

Darwin, Charles, 36
Day-care. See Child care
Department. See also Community of schol-
    ars: colleagues
    chairperson, 28, 93
    committees, 28, 92, 145, 181
    role in promotion and tenure decisions,
        91, 145
Dissertations
    financial support for, 10–11, 13
    research based on, 74
    writing of, 9
Donne, John, 180

Eble, Kenneth E., 39
Eckerman, Carol O., 81–82, 184
Einstein, Albert, 182
Eliot, George, 117, 119
Elnekave, Helen R., 45
Epstein, Joseph, 34
Ethical review committee, 10, 58–59, 79–
    80, 181
Ethics, professional, 12, 187–188. See also
    Research, scientific: ethical standards
Everitt, B. S., 78

Examinations
    grading of, 49
    oral, 45–46
    taking of, 8–9

Faculty. See also Community of scholars;
    Department; Professors
    at academic exercises, 30–31
    academic ranks, 90–94
    committees, 92, 94, 144, 145
    council, 28, 145, 181
    handbook, 27, 92
    responsibilities and autonomy of, 143–
        146
Fielding, Henry, 117
Financial support. See also Grant applica-
    tions
    administration of funds, 150–151
    and choice of research, 74
    responsibilities incurred, 134
    sources of, 10–11, 12, 41, 93–94, 103,
        134–135, 139
        for women and minorities, 10, 109,
            113
Fisher, R. A., 75
Fleming, Alexander, 75
Fordham, Christopher C., 188
Foster, S. L., 9
Fowler, H. W., 7
Fraud, scientific, 53, 150. See also Integ-
    rity; Research, scientific
Freedman, James O., 27, 90, 97, 115
Freud, Sigmund, 8, 36, 184

Gallagher, James J., 175
Glass, Bentley, 180
Gleckner, R. F., 19, 20
Gleitman, Henry, 34
Government, collegial, 20, 26, 41, 144–
    146, 188
Graduate students. See Students
Graduate study, 3–13
    degree requirements, 9–11
    length of, 13
    returning students, 12
Grant applications, 10, 133–139. See also
    Financial support: sources of
    formal approval for, 58–60, 62
    peer reviewing of, 137–138, 169–170
    proposal formats, 103–104, 135–137
    revising, 138–139
Gray, Hanna H., 30

Hall, G. Stanley, 61
Hamburg, David, 156
Harlow, Harry, 156, 158
Hartley, J., 127
Haskett, Josh, 38, 43
Hay, Dale F., 78
Hayne, Don W., 78, 85
Helpers, acknowledgment of, 29–30, 126–127
Hinde, Robert, 156
Holmes, Oliver Wendell, 99, 181
Holton, Gerald, 54
Honor. *See* Ethics, professional; Integrity; Trustworthiness
Honor code, 28, 35, 148
Hull, Clark L., 118

Ideas
  acknowledging source of, 8, 52
  free exchange of, 53–54
Identity, professional, 104–105
Infants, as research subjects, 55
Informed consent, 130. *See also* Research, scientific: with human subjects
  and confidentiality, 55, 56, 59, 67, 70
  documenting, 57
  obtaining, 55–57
  purpose of research, disclosure of, 56
Institutional review board, 10, 59–60
Integrity
  institutional, 151–152
  personal, 4, 54, 91, 147–152
  of science, 10, 28, 52–54, 149–151

Jacob, François, 179
James, William, 8, 36, 133
Job search, 15–21
  application process, 16–18
  interviews, 18
  preparing for, 15–18
  types of openings, 18–21, 101–105
Jones, Lyle V., 91, 146, 147
Journal articles
  peer reviewing of, 168–169, 181
  reading techniques, 6
  revising and resubmitting, 131
  submission of, 130–131
  writing of, 9, 125–129
Journalistic media, dealing with, 175–176
Journals, scientific
  and ethics of research, 63–64
  research preferences of, 74

Kant, Immanuel, 182
Kaplan, Abraham, 80
Kasarda, John D., 38
Kimpton, Lawrence A., 188
Koch, Helen L., 110, 131

Letters of reference, 16–17, 29–30, 92, 170
Lipsitt, Lewis P., 173
Lowman, J., 34

McCarthy, Charles R., 59
McKay, N. Y., 113
McKeachie, W. J., 34
Medawar, Peter B., 74, 80
Meetings, professional
  advantages of attending, 11, 12, 13, 94
  participating in program, 93, 153–155
Mentors. *See also* Students: advising of
  consulting, 21, 93, 112–113, 137, 138
  and intellectual tradition, 4
  serving as, 27, 40–41, 147
Miller, George A., 177
Miller, Neal E., 75–76
Minority persons, 107–113
  financial support for, 10, 109, 113
  mentoring, 112–113

Nabokov, Vladimir, 37
National Academy of Sciences, and honor in science, 52
National Institutes of Health (NIH), 105, 109
National Science Foundation (NSF), 109
Notebooks, keeping of, 118

O'Connor, Maeve, 125, 157

Pavlov, Ivan P., 61
Peer review, 137–138, 167–171, 188
Pelikan, Jaroslav, 36
Plagiarism, 8, 35, 52. *See also* Ethics, professional; Honor code; Integrity
Planning. *See also* Research design
  of a conference, 157–158
  of the day's work, 115–119
  of a symposium, 155
  of a textbook, 161–162
  of time for thought, 119, 182, 183
Plato, 181, 182
Platt, John R., 77
Policy institutes, 175. *See also* Service